Kay Douglas is a qualified psychotherapist who has worked in the helping professions for many years as a social worker, women's refuge worker, counsellor, psycho-therapist and as the co-ordinator of a social service agency that provides support to one-parent families. She has also facilitated grief resolution workshops for people who have experienced the loss of a partner. Kay has a special interest in working with relationship difficulties and women's empowerment. She is passionate about the importance of women's stories.

Kay maintains a private practice and works with a women's centre as a counsellor/psychotherapist. She also co-facilitates men's living without violence programmes. She is the mother of three adult children and step-mother of two children.

INVISIBLE WOUNDS

A Self-Help Guide for Women in Destructive Relationships

KAY DOUGLAS

Published in Great Britain, with new material,
by The Women's Press Ltd, 1996
A member of the Namara Group
34 Great Sutton Street, London EC1V 0LQ

First published in New Zealand by Penguin Books (NZ) Ltd, 1994

Reprinted 2000

British Library Cataloguing-in-Publication Data
A catalogue record for this book is available from the British Library.

ISBN 0 7043 4450 5

Printed and bound in Great Britain by Cox & Wyman Ltd,
Reading, Berkshire

This book is dedicated
to Ellen Rae,
a friend and a mentor
whose tender understanding of my story,
genuine warmth, unquestioning acceptance of me,
love, and enthusiastic encouragement
have touched my life deeply
and helped me to transform my personal pain
into something of value.

It is also dedicated to
the many other women I have met along the way,
whose sheer courage and strength
in the face of tremendous adversity
constantly inspire and humble me,
challenge me to seek
those qualities within myself,
and make me proud to be a
woman.

Contents

Acknowledgements 11

Foreword 15

Introduction 19

1. *The Ways We Are Wounded* 23
2. *The Toll That It Takes* 48
3. *Why Does Our Partner Treat Us This Way?* 68
4. *Seeing The Wider Picture* 75
5. *What Stops Us From Leaving?* 89
6. *Reaching Out for the Support You Need* 95
7. *Reconnecting With Your Self* 109
8. *The Impact On Our Children* 127
9. *Choosing the Right Path* 140
10. *Reclaiming Your Equality Within the Relationship* 150
11. *The Challenge of Breaking Free* 175
12. *Stepping Into a New Beginning* 193
13. *Healing the Wounds* 204
14. *Pearls of Wisdom* 221

Appendices

1. *For Family and Friends* 229
2. *For Counsellors and Other Professionals* 233
3. *Obtaining Court Orders* 237
4. *The Women and Their Stories* 241
5. *Community Resources* 244

Bibliography 253

Index 257

You came into my life
and nothing has ever been the same since.
You touched a special part of me
that no one had ever touched before.
The vulnerable me that longs to be loved.
You lit up my life with laughter,
shared my hopes and dreams,
dried my tears and loved me.
You were a treasured person in my life.

Then things began to change.
The man I knew and loved began to leave,
and in his place was a cold distant stranger
who seemed to want to crush and destroy me.
Where there had been love, warmth and acceptance,
there was coldness and hostility.

Confused and bewildered,
I tried so hard to make things right,
searched for an answer to the question 'why'.
For a long time my memories of what once had been
fed my hope that tender times would come again.
That hope died slowly,
replaced by piercing sorrow
as I descended into the darkness
of total despair.

Leaving you was the hardest thing I ever did,
but I knew I had to do it to survive.
Bewildered, alone, afraid,
I turned my back on all I believed in,
and began the quest
through the darkness, toward light,
to reclaim me.

It takes a long time to pick up the shattered pieces,
and to painstakingly rebuild.
Deep wounds may heal,
but I am not the same. I am changed.
I struggle to come to terms with that.
Will the woman who eventually emerges
somehow learn to trust again?

But there are unexpected gifts.
Sorrow has carved new depth in me.
There is greater understanding and compassion.
And I now know
that the most precious person in my life is me.
I am receiving myself back,
and that gift is all the more precious
because it is truly mine.

– K. D.

Acknowledgements

The vision of *Invisible Wounds* has been shared by many and the creation of it has been a collaborative effort, so there are numerous people to thank.

My deepest gratitude goes to the fifty women who trusted me enough to share the intimate details of their lives. Their experiences, insights and ideas for change and healing enrich this book immeasurably. My thanks also to the thirteen-year-old girl whose memories touchingly remind us of the way the world is through children's eyes.

I would also like to thank sincerely the following professionals who generously gave up their time to share their expertise, discuss the contents of this book and in some cases read parts of the manuscript and offer feedback: Miriam Saphira, Margaret Mourant, Heather McDowell, Barbara Milne, Josie Young, Robyn Rummins and Fay Lilian from the Child Abuse Prevention Society, Louise Chapman and Reese Helmondollar from the North Harbour Men Living Without Violence Collective, Peggy Cleary from Tranx, Marg Dixon from the Women's Refuge Central Office and Patricia Keating (solicitor). My special thanks to Jenette Ford, the co-ordinator of the North Shore Women's Refuge. Working with Jenette has given me an on-going opportunity to discuss issues and gain information. I am particularly grateful for her enthusiasm about *Invisible Wounds* and her faith in my ability to bring it into being.

I also want lovingly to thank a number of friends and family whose encouragement and emotional support during this challenging time in my life has enabled me to carry and complete this worthwhile project. In particular I am grateful to three women who willingly devoted many hours to reading the manuscript and offering suggestions: Gaye Rowley, my writing buddy, for her clarity, skill with words, unwavering faith in this project and the gift of her poem; Ruth Palmer for the loving friendship that nourished me through the good and bad times; and Susan Slater for her optimism and affirmation of my work. I owe a great deal to these women. My thanks also to Joy Pool for her lively, loving spirit; Maureen Chapman for her enthusiastic encouragement; Phyllis Walker for her dependability; Patty Turner for her warmth and laughter; Sue Ransom for her loyality; Marilyn and Tony Anderson for their unfailing hospitality: Gabrielle Kearney for her nurturing and wisdom; Roy Warren for his constant belief in me; Fiona McKay for her sensitive support and input in the early stages of this project; Barbara Cavanagh for being my fellow journeyer and the sister I never had; Wendy-Anne Mathews for her intelligent feedback and compassion; Ellen Rae for helping to fill the empty space in my life left by the recent death of my dear mother; and Brigid McVeigh for continually inspiring me and teaching me that healing is possible. Special thanks to my children Jenny, Angela and Robert Clancy for the gift each of them brings to my life, and for all they have taught me and continue to teach me.

I am also grateful to the many other people who have given their support and the women who informally shared their stories and best wishes with me when they realised the subject of this book.

My sincere thanks to Geoff Walker of Penguin Books for his enthusiasm and good humour; Jane Parkin for her sensitive and skilful editing; and Stephanie Dowrick for the wisdom she shares in the Foreword and her warm validation of my work.

Kay Douglas

Grateful acknowledgement is made to the following works which have been quoted:

Excerpts from *Women Who Run With the Wolves* by Clarissa Pinkola Estes, published by Rider, London, 1992.

Excerpts from *Dreaming the Dark* by Starhawk, published by Mandala, UK, 1990.

Excerpts from *The Prophet* by Kahlil Gibran, published by Heinemann, London, 1955.

Excerpts from *Notes From the Song of Life* by Tolbert McCarroll, published by Celestial Arts, California, 1977.

Excerpts from *The Simple Way* by Lao Tszi, published by Shrine and Wisdom, UK, 1957.

Excerpts from *For Your Own Good* by Alice Miller, published by Virago, London, 1987.

The poem 'Robbery' by Gaye Rowley, from her unpublished private collection.

The poem 'Children Learn What They Live' by Dorothy Law Noble.

Foreword

Kay Douglas has written an extraordinary book about a terrifyingly 'ordinary' phenomenon: emotional abuse of women by men.

This is so ordinary, in fact, that even those living with emotional abuse often tend to confuse it with and excuse it as normal behaviour. If you don't have broken ribs or bruises, if you are not being raped, do you have any right to complain, or any need to act to save your own life?

This painful confusion about what a woman is entitled to expect for herself and from a male partner comes through most powerfully in these pages. This is the magnificent strength of this book. Calmly, persistently and without any equivocation, *Invisible Wounds* shows that denigration, belittlement, contempt, censorship and blaming are not, and never can be, valid expressions of love. They are the expression of an overriding desire for control.

Yet many women – strong intelligent women, kind caretaking women, women who feel confident and decisive in other areas of their lives – may hesitate for many years before taking action to save themselves from an emotionally abusive relationship. And sometimes it may be even harder for women to act when there are no obvious bruises, when it is wounding words or punitive silences that are the weapons of attack.

Kay Douglas takes all the time needed to show why women hesitate so long; why women often continue for years to accept the blame for the very behaviour that hurts them most; why women willingly focus on rescuing their abusing partner rather than saving themselves.

And that is part of what I loved about this book – painful and confronting as it often is to read. Kay Douglas is *patient*. She knows how hard it can be for even the most enlightened woman to face up to the reality that is in front of her eyes, that may be snoring in her bed, when she wishes with all her heart that things were different.

That many men find it difficult – and often impossible – to take any responsibility at all for the emotional pain and distress they cause is not news to most women. That many women feel responsible for the emotional well-being of everyone around them is not news either.

But how this mix-and-match plays its part in the homes and hearts of emotional abusers and their families certainly needs explaining. And it is impossible to escape acknowledging the awful familiarity of the patterns that Kay Douglas lays bare.

Underlying a man's lack of emotional responsibility – for which there is no convincing excuse that I have ever heard – is often sadism. Many men positively and knowingly relish the drama, the tension, the increase in adrenalin that abusing their partner can bring them.

Perhaps they are sorry afterwards, when their heady rush of controlling power subsides. But, as Kay Douglas says, unless they are sorry enough to make substantive changes to their behaviour, the remorse is simply part of a cycle that marks any kind of addiction. In this case, the addiction is to control. The addict must control the people around him, or perhaps his partner only, even if it causes her pain – and sometimes especially if it causes her pain.

He must have her attention on him and his needs. What her separate needs might be, he would rarely know or care. That is the territory of mature love: to know what someone else is feeling and to care about that feeling, even when you do not share it.

I would suggest that any man who is unable to feel or express that kind of mature love, and who is addicted to controlling rather than enhancing the life of his partner, has turned his weak self-image and lack of self-love into a perverse strength to use against his partner. But such an analysis is not part of Kay Douglas' concern.

She sees and knows from her own experience how entrapping it is for any woman to spend her energy exploring *his* motivation, rather than using that same energy to find out what she needs, and how to get it.

Again and again Kay Douglas shows how, without even being aware of what she is doing, a woman will abandon herself to focus on her male partner. *His* needs, *his* moods, *his* boredom, elation, sexual tensions: these all cry out for her attention.

But how will she remain attentive to what is happening to her, and within herself, while her attention is always on him? And how will she grow in self-knowledge and self-love when the demands of the relationship are unbalanced and excessive, and the few rewards are conditional or inauthentic?

It is that absolutely persistent focus on women – and on every woman's right to a life free of abuse and denigration – that makes Kay Douglas' work more than 'just a book'.

Invisible Wounds is the strong, wise companion every woman needs who doubts her right to a life free from emotional abuse, and the shame and self-blame that so often accompany it.

For those feelings of shame and self-blame mean that emotional abuse can be very hard to leave behind, even years after the initial point of recognition.

The guilt and self-blame can seem to make sense: 'If I could only be the wife he needs, he will be nice to me, *then I will have the partner I need*.'

It can be chilling to realise that saving him (from his 'need' to be unkind to you) may be impossible, and that saving him in order to be saved yourself may never be effective. Such an insight may be the moment of a woman's greatest powerlessness and grief, but it is often at that outer reach of our endurance that we can find the strength to act to save ourselves.

While I was reading *Invisible Wounds,* rejoicing that it now exists and raging that it needs to exist, another of my friends died. Sally was fifty-two and the only consolation I can find in the face of her premature death is that she seemed to live those years she did have to the full.

That led me to think about the tragedy of living with emotional abuse, of what it means to exist within a cramped life, a fear-driven life, an unloved, unappreciated and uncherished life.

I feel certain there isn't time for that; not for any one of us. Suffering is part of life, but so is beauty, freedom, self-love and rejoicing. Kay Douglas understands suffering. But her own life, and the rich insights she has gathered for this book, show that she also deeply understands love, courage and freedom. For those are the emotions that can reconnect us with ourselves, and which can and will heal even the deepest of our wounds.

Stephanie Dowrick

Introduction

If you are caught in constant power struggles with your partner and feel hurt, undermined or controlled by him, this book has been written for you. I have written *Invisible Wounds* out of a desire to turn my own experience in a destructive relationship into something of value. As I began to pick up the pieces of my life after leaving the relationship, I needed to make some sense out of what had happened in order to recover. During the process of writing, I have remembered only too well how lost and alone I felt in my relationship: the heartache, the confusion and my constant swings from hope to despair. This is the book I wish I'd had to help me find a way out of that darkness.

During that time what I most needed was to realise that the difficulties in the relationship stemmed from my partner's need to control me, not from my failure to measure up to his standards. My attempts to please him were an impossible task which resulted only in depression, burnout and the loss of my self-esteem. I also needed to understand that constant criticism and rejection take a high toll.

That relationship shattered all my beliefs about my own strength, and my ideals about love and life. As my partner changed from the kind and caring man I had initially grown to love into a cold and punishing man, I felt totally bewildered. He blamed my 'inadequacies' for his change, and in time I believed him. I thought there had to be a logical explanation. I now realise that some men have a driving desire to control their partners at all costs. Love didn't just die instantly because my partner was treating me badly. The emotional bond was strong. It was difficult to give up when I wanted to continue believing the best. I certainly didn't want to face the painful fact that my ecstatic happiness of those early days had been based on an illusion. I remained stuck in the relationship for a long time, swinging between hope and resignation. My fear at taking that irreversible step

19

– leaving him – was like a tangible barrier. I wished I could talk to someone who had been through a similar problem and would understand my dilemma.

The personal stories of fifty such women are woven throughout this book. Their experiences create a rich tapestry of the common and contrasting threads of their lives. Although each of us is unique and separate, we are also connected by our identity as women, and we can draw strength from one another. In writing this book the collective wisdom of these women has been used. All shared valuable insights and ideas for change and healing. They also shared words of encouragement and hope and many heartbreaking memories. Revisiting their time of sorrow and broken dreams was distressing for many of the women, but they went through this willingly in the hope that others would find help and comfort from their stories.

I have kept the focus throughout on the women and their experience, rather than on the men. This is not because the relationship difficulties were the women's fault or responsibility. They were not. I have kept this focus because I believe it is the key to our empowerment. Women are nurturers who are expert at meeting others' needs and desires, while denying their own. As a controlling man demands this attention, and some women's survival may even depend on it, this is a powerful feature of the destructive relationship. To strengthen ourselves we need to change this focus. Throughout this book there are many lists of questions and exercises to assist you in making this change. I am fully aware how difficult it is to tackle exercises when you are under extreme stress, but if you can make the effort, you will begin to feel stronger.

If you are living in a destructive relationship, you may feel isolated, frightened and powerless. Where possible the very best help is caring, empathetic friends, and a skilled professional counsellor who understands the complexities of your situation and is supporting you in regaining your power. This book is intended to complement this care rather than replace it. In situations where it is not possible to have personal support, I hope *Invisible Wounds* may bridge that gap and be a source of information and comfort as well as a means by which to empower yourself to make changes. This book focuses on the dynamics of heterosexual relationships but power struggles can be a feature of any intimate relationship. Therefore women in destructive lesbian relationships may also find it useful.

Invisible Wounds has given those of us who have lived through the pain of a destructive relationship the opportunity to reach out to support other women who are still going through it. Our hope is that when you read this book you will feel validated, supported and less alone at a difficult time in your life. Our love and sincere best wishes are with you.

Kay Douglas

Chapter One

The Ways We Are Wounded

An intimate relationship offers the promise of secure love, companionship, trust and joy. When our partner begins to wound us with cold rejection, cutting words and blazing anger, that early promise fades. Being attacked in these ways is bewildering and painful. We are doing our best, but it seems we're not doing it right. Mounting anxiety tells us things are not as they should be, but we are confused about the real nature of the problem. We become so caught up in our partner's recriminations that we begin to accept the blame for the disharmony between us.

Gradually, the promise of having a fulfilling relationship slips further away, to be replaced by grim coping and striving to please a man who refuses to be pleased.

If you feel manipulated, insulted, criticised or victimised by your partner, you are not alone. Destructive relationships are remarkably common, yet most remain hidden behind closed doors. Many women remain silent about their difficulties because they feel ashamed and are fearful of being met with disbelief, blame or scorn if they confide in other people.

Most of us don't label our partner's destructive behaviour as emotional abuse, but that is often what it is. To many of us, the word 'abuse' brings with it images of severe cruelty and violence, but when put-downs, emotional with-holding, mind games or threats are used systematically to undermine a person, it is just as much a form of abuse as a physical attack. There may be no visible wounds, but our emotions and spirits are being battered and bruised, and this is just as debilitating.

What is abuse?

The abusive relationship is characterised by inequality. *When one partner consistently controls, dominates or intimidates the other by means of manipulative, punishing or forceful behaviour, abuse is occurring.* All couples have power struggles and disagreements at times, but when there is a pattern of control that results in one partner winning on most issues, at the expense of the other's rights, beliefs and desires, that is abuse. Throughout this book the terms 'abuse' and 'control' are used interchangeably because abusive behaviour is meant to control.

A controlling man is usually determined to get his own way. If he doesn't, he retaliates with anger, sulking or rejection. This puts his partner at a considerable disadvantage. To avoid conflict the woman will probably begin to give way on issues which are important to her. In this way her freedom and individuality are gradually eroded.

The man's behaviour may be an unconscious means of control, or he may be quite aware of the power of his abuse. He may believe that it is his partner's job to satisfy him, and that when she fails to do so he is entitled to punish her. Whether it is conscious or not, the result is the same: the woman is being coerced into doing as her partner wants, and in the process is stripped of her rights and identity as an individual.

We often resist acknowledging the destruction in our relationship. Ignoring or denying it can be part of an unconscious survival strategy to keep life bearable on a day-to-day basis. The term 'abuse' makes many of us feel uncomfortable because it seems such a strong word to describe the behaviour of the man we love who may also at times be kind, considerate and loving. But the word abuse defines a pattern of behaviour that is used to maintain control over another. If this is what our partner is doing, we are better off acknowledging it. By becoming clearer about what emotional abuse is, and beginning to view our partner's behaviour in this light, we separate ourselves from the confusion of his blame. We then gain strength to deal with our situation in different ways.

We may fear that having acknowledged the abuse, we will

have no option but to do something immediate about it. This is not so. Understanding is the first step in making any kind of change, but this doesn't mean we have to make sudden decisions or sweeping changes that we feel unwilling or unready for. It is up to each of us to decide what steps, if any, we want to take and how and when we will take them. We each have the right to make those decisions in our own time and way.

We may also feel that the word 'abuse' reflects badly on us. We need to remind ourselves that this term refers to the controlling man's behaviour, not to what we do or to who we are. If our partner is abusing us, it is not our shame: it is his.

The many faces of abuse

The controlling man comes in many forms, from the obviously domineering bully to the smooth, patronising man who constantly implies his partner is inferior. Both attack the woman's self-esteem. Moreover, to achieve control most men will practise a variety of tactics.

On the following pages a number of women share their experiences. Although their stories are very different, you will notice that their feelings of confusion and powerlessness are similar. Some of the events they describe will sound familiar, some will not. When thinking about your own relationship, think about the overall pattern of control. If you are frequently coming off second best and are being manipulated or intimidated into going along with your partner's demands most of the time, then you are probably suffering abuse.

Increasing control

Control may begin early in the relationship but may be so insidious that we are unaware of what we are experiencing. For example, under the guise of the benevolent teacher, ceaseless advice may be given 'for your own good'.

> John was really intelligent and widely read. He introduced me to good books and classical music. At first I was eager to learn, but then it became too much. I'd

ask him a simple question and he'd give me a four-hour
lecture. If I went to move away, he'd accuse me of not
understanding him. If I didn't follow his suggestions,
he'd argue or go into one of those black spaces where I
couldn't get near him. The message was that I belonged
to him and he'd change me to reach my full potential,
as he saw it. After a while I was constantly changing to
suit him, and in doing this I was losing me.

The inequalities in this type of relationship soon become
apparent. As our partner criticises us when we do not perfectly
fit his ideal, the message is, 'You're not good enough as you
are, I will teach you how to be better.' As we begin to realise
the patronising and oppressive nature of our partner's 'help',
we may try to resist his attempts to mould us. This usually
results in further pressure being applied.

Mike expected me to follow his instructions in
everything. His way was right, and mine was wrong. He
even tried to tell me how to clean my teeth! If I didn't
go along with him and do as he wanted, I was rebellious,
pigheaded or ungrateful. Why wouldn't I listen, when
he was only trying to help me?

Gradually the controlling man's advice overshadows
every aspect of our life, directing our choice of clothing,
friends, employment and leisure-time activities. He also puts
pressure on us to give up outside interests, because he 'can't
bear to be apart from us'.

Greg seemed to constantly resent me going out. He was
always saying he was far more available for the
relationship than I was because I was out more, but most
of the time I was just at work. Even then he'd often be
sulky and moody when I got home. In the end it became
easier not to bother doing other things. It wasn't worth
the hassle.

Many controlling men want their partner all to themselves and so see other people as a threat. Reluctant to have
us involved with family and friends, our partner may be
critical of them or offputting if they visit. If he puts us down

and humiliates us in front of other people, we may soon prefer
not to risk socialising anyway.

Control may permeate everything, yet still be subtly
disguised as caring concern. Gradually our freedom is restricted as we are given less opportunity to do what is
important to us.

> Barry wouldn't give me the privacy to pray. He'd walk
> in and ask what I was doing. When was I going to come
> to bed? It was always: 'Come to bed. You've finished
> work, you must be tired. You're frail, you must have your
> rest.'

As our partner takes over more and more of our life, our
confidence and independence are eroded. Often important
decisions are made without any consideration for us.

> Roy just came home from work one afternoon and said,
> 'You can get everything packed. We're leaving
> tomorrow.' I got really upset and cried because I really
> loved that place, but all he said was, 'There's no use
> sitting there crying because we're going. That's it.' I
> didn't have any choice. I just had to go.

Finances are often tightly controlled. There may be
glaringly obvious double standards. We may be given a
meagre, non-negotiable allowance to buy the necessities for
ourselves, the children and the home, while our partner buys
the best of everything for himself. There is money for him to
pursue his interests, yet none for us and the children. He may
even demand that special foods are served to him while
expecting the rest of the family to make do with cheap food.

> As far as David was concerned all the money was his.
> His wages would go into his account, and he had the
> chequebook. I didn't even know how much he earned.
> I'd have to ask for money for food each week, and I had
> to account for everything I spent. If I wanted something
> extra like clothes, I'd just have to go without. There
> wasn't much point in asking, he'd just say no. I'd get
> upset and depressed because I didn't have anything of
> my own, but it never made any difference.

Our partner may insist that we hand our complete wage packet over to him even when we are the main income earner. If his financial schemes go wrong, we may be repeatedly expected to bail him out, even though we have no say in these ventures. Having severely restricted access to finances not only makes us feel powerless, but also makes it more difficult for us to leave the relationship if we choose.

Domestic domination

The controlling man usually believes everything should revolve around him. He expects 'his' woman to serve him stoically in his position of 'master of the house'.

> At five o'clock Frank would walk in and say, 'Where's the dinner?' I'd have it all bubbling on the stove, but I had five small children and often something would go wrong to distract me at the last minute. If it wasn't ready, he'd kick up a fuss and say, 'Right, now I have to drink.' That was his weapon.

The home may be run in a regimented way, like an army camp. Though the man considers the home and children to be woman's work, his authority extends over every aspect of it. The message is, 'This had better come up to my standards, or else.' We are set up for failure as we inevitably fall short of perfection.

> About four o'clock we'd start winding up for the big homecoming. Grant would come in and dust his finger around the ledges and say, 'I can see you've been sitting round all day watching the soaps, this house is a mess', even though it wasn't. He'd ask if I'd changed the sheets and then check to see if I had and the dirty ones had been washed. If the ironing wasn't kept up, he'd thunder and rage and complain to other people.

Enormous pressure can also be placed on us by the expectation that we will keep the children under control and quiet at all times.

> Our son would wake up two or three times a night and nothing would console him. It was terrible. Then Bob

would wake up and he'd get furious. I remember him shouting, 'If you don't shut that fucking kid up, I'm going to throw it through the wall.' My hands started to shake and I knew I had to get out of there, so I put the baby in the pushchair and walked the streets from one until three o'clock in the morning. I had to do that on several occasions.

The need to possess

Many controlling men are excessively possessive, but this may begin in subtle ways.

Kevin would do everything for me. He'd run my bath, wash me, dry me, clean my teeth, put me into a warm bed, dress me, he'd even walk down the hallway with me if I wanted to go to the toilet in the night.

At first we may be flattered that this man wants to devote himself so entirely to every aspect of our life. He seems so intensely interested in our welfare that we naturally take this as a sign of affection. But after a while these deceptively innocent gestures became suffocating. The unspoken message is, 'You're mine.'

Peter would sit in a chair facing the door so that everyone that came in was under his surveillance. He was always the one to answer the door and the phone, and would quite often not pass important messages on to me. It got to the stage where I couldn't even have a phone call without him standing beside me or wanting me to sit on his knee so he could hear the whole conversation too. The windows were being closed as quickly as I opened them, and so was the front door. I felt like a prisoner in my own house.

Our possessive partner may become increasingly suspicious, watching us constantly, accusing us of being deceitful or unfaithful and expecting us to account for every minute we are away from him.

Jeff was very jealous. He always thought that his friends would move in on me, or that I was inviting them to. I had to be constantly aware not to sit too close to any of them, to look away or down rather than directly at them, and not to go round to see any of the wives if their husbands were home. I wasn't even supposed to talk when his friends were visiting, and if I did he'd glare at me. I just had to sit there.

Many possessive men harass and interrogate their partners about imagined infidelities. Fearful of these outbursts, we may restrict our contact with others, but the accusations continue regardless. Our partner's jealousy can even extend to the children, whom he may see as rivals who compete with him for our attention.

Craig would get really uptight when he saw me giving attention to our daughter. He'd even try to stop me going to her when she cried at night when she was a baby. He honestly believed she was trying to come between us, even when she was only one month old.

His obsession may gradually extend to every area of our life.

Vince went through absolutely everything of mine – my letters, accounts, clothing and personal possessions of every type. He'd spy on me and listen at doors.

This man doesn't take a partner, he takes a hostage.

Relentless demands

For some men, no amount of effort, attention, care, love or sex will ever be enough. The demands are endless.

Brett would hound me on the phone a lot. I had a very good job working for a senior partner in a law firm. I was extremely busy, and didn't have time to talk on the phone. I'd try to cut the conversation down by explaining I had urgent work to do. And he'd say, 'Aren't I important in your life? Can't you spend a few minutes talking to me?' If I didn't, he'd be furious and refuse to forgive me. He always managed to twist things around so that he was the one being short-changed and hurt, because I wasn't there for him every minute of the day.

We are expected to prove our love by giving our partner endless attention. Our needs are of little consequence. As he uses punishing behaviour to manipulate us into giving him the attention he craves, our partner's unmistakable message is, 'I am the important one.'

> I'd arrive home exhausted from work and Ray would immediately launch into a technical lesson on the computer. If I dared to suggest I'd rather get dinner, he'd go cold and accuse me of being ignorant, and end up sulking for days. Even if I watched for a while he'd still get nasty and sulky when I called a halt. Really, I just couldn't win.

Subtle set-ups

A controlling man's tactics for undermining his partner can be so subtle that we are often completely unaware of them.

> I had a weight problem, but whenever I made an effort to diet Wayne would sabotage me every time by buying chocolate bars. It was the only time he ever bought chocolate home. I was really addicted to chocolate, so it was like slow torture. I was trying to improve my appearance, but I got the distinct impression that he didn't want me to look better.

Sometimes our partner plays games which leave us feeling frustrated and infuriated. These incidents of control may seem relatively harmless but nevertheless the strings are being pulled and we are being manoeuvred into a put-down position.

> Garry had a very warped sense of humour and he used to like playing with me and upsetting me. One night he came home and told me he'd been sacked for stealing. I was absolutely beside myself. No job, bills and a big mortgage, and we were building a house. The next night, after all my panic, he told me he was having me on. I was really upset but according to him, I had no sense of humour because I didn't think it was funny.

Our partner may manipulate us into behaving in a certain way, and then blame us for our reaction.

> The only time Mike would approach me for a cuddle was when I was frazzled: the kids were in the bath or I was getting dinner and we were running late. It was like he picked the most inopportune times, and then if I didn't respond he'd get angry and accuse me of never wanting to cuddle him. Any other time he wouldn't approach.

Often we are set up by our partner so he has an excuse to berate us for our 'inadequacies'.

> Tim had an affair with another woman and that absolutely knocked me. I nearly had a breakdown over it. We agreed to put it in the past and to try again, and I asked him not to mention her. But we'd be in bed together and he'd drop in her name. I was still so raw that I'd just freak out. I'd get really turned off and wouldn't want to make love. Then he'd get all huffy with me, and turn it round to make it seem like my fault.

We experience a nagging sense of frustration because somehow, no matter what we do, we are made to feel in the wrong. The rules change constantly. What pleased our partner yesterday is unacceptable today. When we cannot put our finger on exactly what is happening, we are unable to deal with it.

Belittling and undermining

As our controlling partner has a need to feel superior to his partner, he often ignores or discredits our achievements. In belittling us he is saying, 'You do not count. You will never be as important as me.' We are left feeling self-doubting, insignificant and diminished as a person.

> It took me three years to get to the level where I won a championship with my horse. I was absolutely ecstatic. Over the moon! I went home with a cup and sash and said, 'Look what I've won', and all Russell said was, 'You're in front of the television.'

To tighten his authority over the family, our controlling partner may gradually undermine us by convincing us we are an inadequate parent.

> The one thing I'd held on to was that everyone always said I was a good mother. Then Paul said that my way of parenting was wrong. I was too soft. My children should not talk at the dinner table. Their rooms were to be kept spotless, and they were to do as they were told instantly. No questions asked. When he told me I wasn't a good parent, it was like he was taking away the last thing I felt good about. I remember thinking, If I'm doing that wrong too, then there's nothing left.

The silent treatment

The punishment of silence is a powerful means of control over a woman, especially when it is accompanied by blatant hostility. Living with frequent episodes of sulky silence is extremely stressful and demoralising. An unbearable tension is created by our partner's black moods. This evokes strong feelings of helplessness, abandonment, frustration and fear in us.

> I'd do something that upset Nigel, like not wanting to have sex, and he'd retaliate by sulking for days. He'd go right into himself and become very, very black and seething. I hated it, it would really get me down. Just to break the silence I'd often end up apologising and make up by initiating sex, but I hated myself for it.

Our partner's silence can manipulate us into compliance. When we know from past experience that our partner will withdraw from us if we say or do anything he disapproves of, we are likely to resort to silent submission. Some men totally reject their partner for days, weeks or even years. The clear message is, 'You are unworthy of my attention.'

> For weeks on end Phil wouldn't acknowledge my existence in any way. He refused to speak or even look at me. It drove me absolutely crazy. Sometimes I felt so desperate for affection I'd ask for a hug and he'd get

angry and say, 'Don't ask, just take one.' Then if I did, he'd just stand there rigidly with his hands by his sides. If I tried to make love he'd either lie there without moving and let it all happen, or he'd say, 'Leave me alone', coldly and finally. When I tried to discuss what was happening he'd tell me to fuck off. If I didn't go, he'd push me out of the room and shut the door in my face, even though it was my house. It was total powerlessness and humiliation.

It can be excruciatingly painful to live with a partner's indifference or cold contempt. We all rely on those around us to give us a sense of who we are. Without opening his mouth, our partner continually communicates to us that he considers us worthless. When we are starved for affection and deprived of recognition, it is like living in an emotional desert. This dehumanising behaviour shatters our self-esteem. Indifference and cold contempt create deep wounds.

When I went into labour I didn't even tell Des for the first few hours because he wasn't speaking to me. When I finally asked him to take me to the hospital he seemed really put out and hostile. He never spoke a word all the way there. Then at the hospital he totally ignored me. He sat in the chair that was the furthest away, put his head back and pretended to sleep. Then he read magazines and I remember just before our son was born he was walking past the bottom of the bed to get another magazine. As he was born Des was standing there looking at him, but he never even looked at me. He later told me I had excluded him from the birth process.

Mind games and manipulation

Our controlling partner is often a master at twisting the facts around to suit himself. The object of the exercise is to blame us for all the problems while at the same time ensuring that he appears innocent. To this end, our partner may contradict himself, change the story of past events or blatantly deny events happened at all. Naturally, if our perceptions of reality are invalidated repeatedly, we soon begin to feel confused.

Chris would say, 'Get yourself ready, and when I come at twelve-thirty we'll go out for lunch.' Then he'd come home at eight o'clock at night and say, 'Why aren't you ready?' When I'd tell him he was supposed to be home at twelve-thirty, he'd insist that I had it wrong. He'd be so adamant that I'd have to stop and think, but you couldn't argue with him. It happened so often that it got to the point where I wasn't sure what I was hearing or what I believed any more.

The message is, 'You're crazy', and this is often verbalised. Many tactics may be used to add to our confusion. Distraction is an excellent way to avoid confrontation. To create a smoke screen, our partner may accuse us of the very behaviour he is indulging in, block communication by getting angry, or bait us with false accusations which we then try unsuccessfully to counteract. After an episode of this kind of 'communication', we are left totally frustrated and disempowered.

I'd try to discuss something rationally with Murray and he'd immediately start to shout over the top of me, 'You're being aggressive. Look at you. Listen to yourself. I'm not discussing anything with you while you're behaving like this.' It didn't matter which way I approached it, it was the same every time. I never got off base one.

We may also be deprived of sleep as our partner harasses us and argues over trivialities late into the night.

Don would ask me what was wrong, and I'd tell him nothing was, but he wouldn't accept that. He'd go on and on about it, until eventually I'd go to bed, and then he'd come and turn the light on and keep at me: 'You haven't told me what's wrong. You're not going to bed on an argument.' I'd say, 'I'm not arguing. The only thing that's wrong is that you're hounding me.' Then he'd say, 'It's all in your head. You're imagining it.' I started to think there was something wrong with me. Maybe I was going crazy.

Psychological abuse is usually part of an attempt to gain control rather than to undermine our sanity deliberately, although occasionally that is our partner's objective. Either way, we often begin to discount our view of reality in favour of the false one our partner is creating. As his brainwashing continues, we may become increasingly afraid we are losing our sanity.

Dr Jekyll and Mr Hyde

A surprising number of controlling men have two very distinct sides to their personality: the charming, caring man, and the cold, abusive one. Of course it is the charming side of this man that we initially meet and grow to love.

> At first everything was just wonderful. I couldn't believe my luck. I'd met this caring and intelligent man. Paul brought such joy into my life, and so much laughter. When we made plans for the future I honestly thought we were going to be so happy together. He seemed so sincere and gentle, I'd have trusted him with my life.

When we are safely involved, our partner has less need to impress. He begins to reveal the darker side of his personality. When he doesn't get his own way, he may have sudden temper tantrums or lapse into hostile silences. Where once he was an ardent and attentive lover, he may now sometimes suddenly become selfish or forceful. Before long we don't know what to expect. At times our partner is delightful, but then he will change for little or no reason and seem intent on making our lives an absolute misery. This unpredictable switching back and forth keeps us constantly on edge. Of course we want to believe that the kind and caring side of our partner, the one we fell in love with, is the 'real' man.

> Warren would be totally withdrawn and wouldn't speak to me for days, and then we'd go out and he'd become this happy and bright 'life and soul of the party' person. He'd be his old charming self in front of everyone and I'd start to relax and think, 'Thank God he's snapped out of it.' Then the minute we got into the car he'd just cut me dead again. No particular reason, except now there was no one to impress. It was devastating.

Usually our partner maintains his 'good guy' image in front of other people, so they continue to believe he is as he appears. Therefore we often have the added distress of knowing we will not be believed if we tell others about our partner's hurtful attacks. Because he presents so well, and we may be over-wrought and emotional, others are more likely to believe that we are the one who is difficult to live with!

Typically this type of man tends to be aware of just how far he can push his partner. If he senses we are about to leave, he will usually use his charm to seduce us into changing our mind.

Words that wound

Insulting, sarcastic and cutting words are powerful weapons. They can be used to mock, ridicule, punish and persecute a woman.

> We were on a cycling holiday. It was very early on Christmas morning and as we pedalled along I was in absolute seventh heaven. It was so beautiful, I felt like all my dreams had come true. I was singing at the top of my voice when suddenly Barry just turned on me and really put me down. The tone of his voice was so harsh and the words so scathing, I was really crushed. He was so nasty about my singing, though I know I do sing in tune. In reality he was the one that couldn't sing, but I'd never have done that to him.

At first we may be able to shrug off criticism and see it as an attack that is not based on truth. However, before long our partner's cruel words begin to take their toll, and our defences and confidence inevitably begin to crumble.

> Pete would scream at me that I was fat and stupid, a useless and uncaring person, a bad wife and mother. Put me down as much as he possibly could, and then ignore me for about three days, while I went around thinking I must be this really bad person. He convinced me that I was such a bad mother that being with my children was actually detrimental to their welfare. I honestly believed that.

A man who uses verbal abuse may criticise every part of his partner's being: our behaviour, opinions, competence, intelligence and appearance.

> I'd always been quite skinny, with absolutely no breasts. According to John my body was the absolute pits. I was worthless because I had no tits. He would still fondle my breasts to get off on them, though. He used to put down every single part of my body, and say how ugly it was, and I believed him. He went through the lot. It's funny. I finally realised the truth when he got down to criticising my feet: I'd always known I had cute, nicely shaped feet. It was then I instantly realised he was doing this to keep me down.

Angry outbursts

Using anger to intimidate and control others is abusive. Living with irrational anger is like living in an emotional minefield. We are never certain when the next blow-up is going to occur. This keeps us in a constant state of anxiety as we try to anticipate, prevent and cope with our partner's outbursts.

Angry explosions are frightening enough to live with, but when that is combined with fist-pounding, dish- and furniture-breaking and wall-punching, it becomes a terrifying reminder of the controlling man's power over us. The message is, 'Next time it could be you.'

> Tony was a big and powerful man, and he punched a lot of holes in the walls. There were many times when his fist was only inches away from me. I was constantly trying to keep the peace, keep it quiet and not rock the boat so he wouldn't blow up.

Scare tactics are a form of psychological abuse. Women are often intimidated into submission with the use of threats. We have all heard stories about the vicious injuries some men inflict on their partners. Even if our partner is only threatening violence, we have no doubt that the consequences of non-compliance could be severe.

Physical assaults can include restraining, spitting, pushing, shaking, slapping, hair-pulling, throwing objects or kicking. Initially we may not realise the seriousness of such incidents, but over time these tactics can escalate into severe physical assaults. Sometimes the first beating may occur suddenly after years in the relationship.

> We'd been married six years the first time Tony hit me. He was outside going mad at the dogs, and I went out and told him what I thought about it. The next thing I knew, I came to on the kitchen floor. I got such a shock. He'd really taken to me.

The abusive man usually claims his partner provoked him. *No provocation is justification for violence. Violence is against the law. No woman has to put up with it.*

After the first attack we naturally live in fear of the next. Even if we are never attacked again, the memory of that first time is enough to make us wary of any confrontation in the future. In fact it is rare for physical violence to be limited to one attack. Usually it is the beginning of an escalating pattern of physical abuse.

> After I got pregnant everything seemed so much better. Stuart had stopped hitting me and we were getting on much better. Because there was going to be another life involved I decided to speak to him about his drinking. When I did, he didn't say anything, he just looked at me. Didn't take his eyes off mine, as he punched me full fist in the stomach. I was standing at the top of the stairs, and I still remember the view as I tumbled down: it was like I was seeing everything in slow motion. He left, and when I could I crawled to the car and drove myself to the doctor. I lost my little girl. She would have been five this year. I've never seen Stuart since.

Domination in the bedroom

Oppression, conflict and humiliation are often a feature of the sexual relationship with a controlling man. To assert his dominance and power, he may practise many forms of sexual abuse. Often he expects us to be there to meet his needs

whenever, wherever and however he chooses; our body may
be treated as if it were his possession. He may make suggestive
comments about other women, compare us unfavourably to
them, imply or threaten that he will go elsewhere for sex, or
do so. Sexual activity may be exclusively on his terms and
demanded 'as of right', without consideration for our feelings
or desires. Our partner may put endless pressure on us about
the frequency of sex, berating and bullying us until he has
his way.

> According to Kim it was never appropriate to say no to
> sex. Not only was I expected to give him sex whenever
> he wanted it, I was expected to enjoy it and reach a
> climax as well. If I did, he'd be nice to me afterwards,
> but if I wasn't responsive enough he'd go on and on
> about how I wasn't normal, had big problems sexually,
> and tell me I needed to go to counselling. It used to upset
> me, so I'd really try hard to please him.

As our sexuality is a unique part of ourselves, it is perfectly
appropriate as it is. Naturally we are particularly vulnerable
to criticism in this area, but no one has the right to judge us
or tell us how we 'should' be. Our controlling partner's self-
serving rules and unrealistic expectations can leave us no
room to know or express our own sexuality. Without free
choice, sex becomes a time of struggle that reminds us of our
powerlessness and our partner's apparent lack of regard for
us.

> If he wanted sex, Grant's signal was to come up when I
> was at the bench and pinch my nipples. I hated it and
> it hurt. I'd always tell him, 'Don't do it, I don't like it.'
> And he'd say, 'You do. You find it a turn-on.' This went
> on for years. If I didn't want sex he'd blame me and slam
> doors, scream abuse, sulk or go out drinking with the
> boys. Heavy emotional blackmail! A lot of the time I gave
> in just for peace. I became very effective at just lying
> there and not feeling anything at all. Faking it got it over
> even quicker, but in the long term I lost myself, and my
> self-esteem, by doing this.

When a woman is continually badgered, bullied or

punished into having sex, and put down for her 'perform-ance', she will lose her sex drive and shut down. This is natural self-protection. Usually the controlling man expects his partner to continue to be responsive toward him, even straight after an episode of abuse. When we understandably find this difficult, he begins another round of recriminations which only repel us further. In theory a woman has the right to say 'No' to touching and sex that she does not want, but if the outcome is hostility and ill-treatment, we may feel we have have little or no choice but to concede.

Insisting on sex is not the only way to claim power over a woman. Withholding can also be used. We may be ridiculed for wanting sex or refused it in a nasty, cutting way. Foreplay may be denied and we may be put down and humiliated if we dare to ask for it. Our partner may completely ignore us during the sex act, as if we were an object rather than a human being with feelings.

> Sometimes Mark would deliberately arouse me, then suddenly pull away and just turn his back on me. I'd be left totally up in the air, not even knowing what I'd done wrong. If I tried to ask him, he'd just get up without speaking and go and sleep in another room, and I'd be left crying and alone. Later he'd act like I'd done something bad to him.

Demanding or withholding, the controlling man is in charge and we are made to feel powerless.

If a person's need for sex is excessive, compulsive and insatiable, it may fall into the category of an addiction. This means sex is used as a temporary means of releasing stress and decreasing anxieties, in a similar way to the addictive use of alcohol or drugs. To the man addicted to sex, the woman is his 'fix', so it is essential that he maintains control over her. In this situation any attempts we make to refuse sex are liable to be met with extreme anger and sometimes even rape.

> There was no way I could say no to sex. It was very uncomplicated. If I didn't concede, Bob would force me. He was a very strong man, and he seemed to think that this was what this love thing was all about.

It is not uncommon for women in abusive relationships to be forced to have sex against their will. Even if the woman has recently given birth and has stitches that will rupture, this may not deter her partner. She may be coerced or forced into participating in sexual practices that she finds offensive, or made to have sex in front of her children or with other men. Objects may be inserted into her vagina or anus. She may be threatened with violence, physically injured during sex, or sex may be used as a brutal and punishing display of power.

> I had an ectopic pregnancy and it ruptured, and when they operated they found I had a cyst as well, so it was a major operation. When I came home from hospital I was in so much pain I couldn't even walk. My partner was in a really bad mood and raised his belt to our one-year-old baby. I intervened to draw the attention onto myself so he didn't take it out on her. He sent her to her room, screamed at me, and then threw me on the bed and raped me. He'd call it making love. He did so much damage and I was in such a bad way, I had to call the doctor.

Pay-backs and punishments

Using punishing behaviour against a partner is a form of manipulation that soon encourages compliance. There are countless ways of punishing a person for real or imagined 'misdemeanours', including bullying, sulking or anger. The underlying message is, 'Do it my way, or you'll be sorry' – and we soon learn this is so.

> When James was angry with me he'd drive recklessly in the car, and I'd find that absolutely terrifying. Every time I asked him to slow down he'd just go faster. I hated it. I felt absolutely powerless.

Retaliation can be extremely subtle.

> My possessions were constantly getting broken by Keith. At first I believed these were just accidents, and then I thought, 'No, not this often. It's deliberate. If he can't destroy me, he'll destroy my property.'

Passive resistance is often used to make us pay.

> We'd have something to go to together, and at the very last moment Frank would refuse to go. When he didn't go to a family wedding that was his way of getting at me. He knew I would be terribly embarrassed and that was my punishment.

Our efforts may be met with senseless persecution.

> I was putting the washing on the line and Dave was getting annoyed because I was taking too long and he wanted to go out, so he picked up a container of car oil and threw it all over the washing, sheets and all. Then he told me, 'If you want something to do, you can wash that again, can't you?' Then I just had to go with him and the washing had to stay on the line as it was. I didn't dare say anything.

Sometimes punishment is vindictive and dangerous.

> It was our first night in Bangkok. We went out to dinner and everything was fine until I unintentionally made some comment that upset John. He turned on me, told me to fuck off and stormed off. I didn't have the faintest idea how to get back to the hotel in the dark. I ran after him, pleading with him not to leave me, but he just walked faster and kept swearing at me. I was absolutely terrified. I had no option but to follow him, and he walked for almost two hours with me frantically trying to keep up, begging him to stop. I was absolutely distraught. Now I can see he had me right where he wanted me.

Often the supposed reason for our partner's anger is just an excuse to lash out.

> I did a little thing wrong, like forgetting to let the water out of the bath, and there was a blow-up and Carl threatened to slit my horse's throat. I was really scared because he didn't usually make threats. He was more likely just to go and do it. The next day I secretly moved her right out of the area.

Threatening to harm us, or a person or animal that we love, evokes real fear. Violence is the ultimate punishment and these threats should always be taken seriously. (See 'Strategies for ensuring your safety . . .', p. 187.)

Setting children against their mother

While some controlling men see their children as competitors for our attention, others see them as allies in their fight against us. Our partner may undermine our authority over our children by deliberately setting them against us. He may seduce them to his 'side' with gifts, money and attention; treat them as his confidants, or set them up in a role that rivals ours.

> One day Nigel just announced, 'You're not having a chequebook any more. From now on Sharleen is going to do all the shopping. I've opened a cheque account in her name, and I'll give her the housekeeping money each week.' Our daughter was seventeen at that stage. It was like he was treating her as his wife.

Needless to say it is extremely destructive for children to have to cope with the stress of divided loyalties. (See 'The Impact On Our Children', Chapter 8.)

Sometimes our partner may begin to sexualise his relationship with our child by invading her personal privacy, making frequent comments about her emerging sexuality or making sexually suggestive remarks. These and other forms of sexual abuse are discussed in 'Child abuse', p. 136.

Tyrannical rule

Some abusive men consider themselves the undisputed head of the household. They rule with an iron hand.

> We'd be all eating silently at the table and the next thing Peter's fist would crash down and all the plates would jump, and he'd bellow at my son for some small thing like chewing with his mouth open. It was so unexpected, Tony would burst into tears and then Peter would stand

over him and shout, 'I'll give you something to cry about if you don't stop.' My heart would go out to this little boy who was being absolutely terrorised and I'd try to protect him by calming Peter down, even though I was angry at him for doing it.

The whole family may feel totally at the mercy of this man's behaviour and live in terror of his outbursts.

If our son dirtied himself, Alan would take him upstairs, lock the bathroom door and rub his dirty underwear all over his face. He'd tell our son he'd never amount to anything in his life; all he was fit for was cleaning toilets. I'd bang on the door and try to bash it down, desperate to get in. Afterwards Alan would storm out of the house and I'd rush to our son and cuddle him and tell him that Daddy didn't mean it, that he loved him and was just having a bad time at the moment. Maybe my reaction just made it worse by confusing the child. I don't know.

Although very different, these stories about the many faces of abuse have one thing in common: the man has a need to control. You may feel that your own situation is not as bad or extreme but, even if it is not, be careful not to invalidate your own pain. There will always be others worse off than ourselves, but that does not make our own situation any less destructive to us. No matter how small the abusive incidents we experience, they deserve to be taken seriously if they are causing us distress.

In considering your situation it is also important to realise that control tactics usually escalate over time. Abuse that starts out as verbal attacks can progress to punching holes in walls and may eventually spill over into physical violence. Most of the more shocking episodes of abuse described in this chapter were inflicted by men who started out as apparently caring partners, who began to exercise control in small ways and progressed to major abuse over time.

Answering the following questions will help you to clarify your situation.

Does your partner . . .

- Criticise you, call you names or belittle the things you do?
- Demand increasing amounts of your time, energy, attention or affection?
- Insist on having his own way on most issues?
- Expect you to be with him constantly, and resent any time you spend pursuing your own interests or seeing other people?
- Keep control of the money and give you an inadequate allowance?
- Treat you with hostile silence and cold contempt for long periods?
- Use punishing behaviour to manipulate you into complying with his demands?
- Harass you or use standover tactics to get his own way?
- Fly into sudden, irrational tempers for little or no reason, then blame these outbursts on you?
- Frighten you by smashing possessions?
- Threaten to harm you or the people you love?
- Slap, shove, shake, pull your hair, kick or punch you?
- Show excessive jealousy and accuse you unjustly of flirting or having affairs?
- Coerce you into having sex when you don't want to, or participating in sexual practices that you don't feel comfortable with?
- Constantly refuse to take responsibility for his destructive behaviour?
- Deny events happened as they did, or turn them around so that he can blame you for them?
- Withhold emotional support, even when you have a major crisis to deal with like a death in the family?
- Make jokes at your expense or deliberately humiliate you in front of others?
- Pretend to be kind and caring toward you in front of others but treat you badly when you are alone together?
- Undermine your relationship with your children?
- Deprive you of sleep by arguing late into the night?

- Improve his behaviour if he thinks he may lose you but resume his abuse when he knows the danger has passed?

If you have answered 'yes' to some or many of these questions, you may be feeling distressed. You may be shocked, angry or terrified of the implications for your future now you are facing the truth. You may also feel a sense of relief that suddenly you can begin to identify the source of your pain more accurately. If possible, release these feelings by expressing them to a friend or writing about them. (See Choosing a confidant', p. 97 and 'The release of writing', p. 124.)

Exercise: Naming the abuse

The first step in regaining control of your life is to stop, stand back and begin consciously to identify the abuse in your relationship.

In a destructive relationship when a difficulty occurs, there are often issues of control underlying what is happening. The next time there is a problem with your partner, ask yourself three questions:

- What is really happening here?
- Is this issue about my partner's need to control, punish or undermine me?
- How can I protect myself in this situation now?

These questions will help you gain awareness, but this is only the first step. Be cautious about confronting your partner too quickly. Rather than taking a sudden stand which you cannot sustain, it is best to continue reading, gain a deeper understanding about what is happening, think through your options and develop new skills to deal with your situation.

Chapter Two

The Toll That It Takes

You wormed your way into my mind, and burgled my virtue.
You turned all the mirrors askew inside my head
And I lost my way.
You dropped a stolen flower on my bed, to pacify me
And turned everything around so completely
That I thought I was the intruder.

– 'Robbery', Gaye Rowley

Abuse is so painful to live with that most of us cope by denying its impact. This was certainly my experience. By excusing my partner's behaviour and pretending I was coping, I created an increasingly damaging illusion. My self-deception prevented me from facing up to just how betrayed, burdened and unloved I was feeling. It kept me hanging in there, trying, while my best efforts were treated with contempt. And it allowed me to keep my head buried in the sand for so long that I became emotionally bankrupt.

As other women have shared their experiences of controlling relationships with me, I have been struck by the remarkable similarities in the way the abuse affected us. I have found it reassuring to realise that the feelings and reactions I had were shared by many other women who had lived with controlling men.

As we embarked on our relationships, many of us willingly, if naively, agreed to most of our partner's demands, without realising the long-term implications of doing so. As his pressure to comply grew, we began to take a stand, but standing our ground soon became exhausting. We found that even if we won a point, our partner usually made us regret it. Over time our lives became a choice between concession and conflict – and concession often became the less painful option. Because we wanted to have a good relationship with our partner, we were willing to work at it. And work we did! To make it seem worthwhile we learned to focus on the good times and play down the bad.

As we were treated increasingly harshly, we tried to weave our way more carefully through the emotional minefield we lived in, but we were caught out time and again by the unexpected. We became watchful, trying to anticipate our partner's moods. His reactions were often so unpredictable that we felt constantly on edge. We became apprehensive and guarded, afraid of unwittingly upsetting him. Soon more and more of our energy revolved around trying to prevent the dreaded episodes which left us feeling shattered and worthless. Our lives became a series of manoeuvres designed to organise, pacify, diffuse and counteract.

Our partner told us that we were the ones at fault, and we decided it must be so. Why else would he treat us this way? We became hard on ourselves: self-blaming, critical and condemning. We tried harder to please, and our self-esteem slipped even lower as we were given the message that we still did not measure up.

It is often the strongest women who stay the longest in abusive relationships. Determined not to give up, we pride ourselves on our ability to cope with the stress. As we constantly draw on our reserves of energy, personal sacrifices go unnoticed and the high cost unacknowledged. This is the danger for us all. It is easy to get so involved in coping that we lose sight of what our coping is doing to us.

The impact of abuse on identity, emotions, behaviour and health will be explored in this chapter. At the end of each section, there is a list of questions to consider. Moving out of denial to count the cost is painful but empowering. Facing the truth about your distress is a major step towards improving your situation.

The impact on identity

The controlling man considers himself more important than his partner. His needs, desires, opinions and rights take precedence over ours. To maintain control, he stifles our self-expression and undermines our sense of personal power. Trying to maintain a strong and separate identity while living in this situation is like fighting a losing battle.

As the controlling man takes much more than he gives, his needs are met at our expense: as he gains, we lose. Our losses are many but the most profound is the loss of our sense of self. Along with this we also lose our creativity, self-esteem, freedom and rights.

Loss of self

With our attention focused outwards on our demanding partner, we begin to lose touch with who we are and what is important to us. As our partner short-changes us, we also short-change ourselves.

- Our needs are rejected, so we deny them.
- Our desires are ignored, so we dismiss them.
- Our opinions are invalidated, so we discard them.
- Our values are dishonoured, so we abandon them.
- Our words are twisted, so we remain silent.
- Our feelings are too painful, so we numb them.

In these ways we gradually become a stranger to ourselves and may eventually slide into depression.

> I went in this hollow space where I felt as if I wasn't even real. Paul was acting like I didn't exist. He wouldn't speak to me or answer me, and walked past me as if I wasn't there. After a while it made me feel really strange. The silence would ring in my ears and I felt numb and blank, like I was living in a vacuum where I was invisible.

Loss of creativity

Our creativity is our unique way of expressing our identity in the world. Any activity that we enjoy because it gives us a deep sense of satisfaction is creative. We may express our creativity in the way we care for our children, prepare food, create a home or garden, or through music, writing, dance, handcrafts or art. The pleasure we gain from creating feeds our spirit. When our creativity stops flowing, a vital part of us begins to wither.

> Over time I just lost interest in all the things I used to enjoy doing. I had no concentration and I couldn't seem to action things in the same way. My ideas dried up and I couldn't get enthusiastic about anything. I used to love to sew, but I'd get halfway through something and I'd think, 'What's the use?' There just didn't seem to be any point to it any more.

Loss of self-esteem

Our partner is in a position to know us better than perhaps any other. Therefore his rejection and criticism have real power to hurt us. When we offer him our best and are given the message that it is of little or no value, the effect is devastating.

> I felt like a rotten tomato that had been flung across the room and was just splattered against the wall, with all my life dribbling down. Absolutely no good. I'd offered him everything I had – myself, a home, money and even a ready-made family – and none of it was good enough.

We have the right to expect our partner to acknowledge us as a worthwhile human being. If he refuses to do that, then it is essential we find other people who will affirm our worth. We can take comfort in the fact that obviously our partner does not know us as well as he thinks. If he did, he would appreciate us as the special person we are.

Loss of freedom and rights

Our controlling partners are threatened by our independence. To maintain their domination, they curtail our freedom and restrict our rights. Some do this extremely subtly, by constantly displaying their irritation whenever their partner takes her attention off him to pursue her own interests. Other men set autocratic rules and punish their partners for disobeying them. Either way, our partner is limiting our self expression and ensuring that our world is getting smaller and we are becoming more dependent on him.

> He'd get sulky and shitty if I put the television on during the day, so I'd rush to turn it off if he got home. Then he started checking when he got home to see if it was warm, and if it was he'd get really angry, so I didn't dare put it on at all. It just wasn't worth it.

Our partner likes to see himself as being in charge of our lives. To show us who's boss, he often denies us the things we want. Some of us are intimidated into relinquishing our rights over issues as important as our own bodies, our life choices, our finances and our contact with our family. In reality we have the right to make decisions about these things for ourselves. (See 'Acknowledge your rights', p. 160.)

Questions to consider: Do you . . .

- Feel out of touch with your feelings, desires and needs?
- Feel undermined as a person, as though the things that are important to you don't count?
- Behave less confidently at home than you do in the outside world?
- Face disapproval from your partner whenever you attempt to spend time with friends and family, or pursue your interests outside the home?

The emotional impact

It may seem to other people that we are coping with our lives so well. We put on a brave face to hide our frightening inner turmoil. Our feelings are intense, conflicting and changeable. Identifying our feelings can help to ease the confusion. (See 'The importance of feelings', p. 115.) Among the tangle of their many emotions, most women experience the following six feelings: fear, shame, guilt, anger, sadness and confusion.

Fear

Numerous fears may plague us. We fear for our uncertain future. We feel intimidated or even terrified by our partner's behaviour. We dread other's disapproval of our situation. We are afraid we are going crazy. Our fear may be a throbbing terror, or it may be a low-level, haunting anxiety that we are scarcely aware of because it has become our constant companion. Gradually our fears can escalate into feelings of panic.

> I seemed to be so afraid, and yet I wasn't even sure why. I think it was mainly that I never knew what to expect. Things seemed to happen so quickly and Brett was so unpredictable. One minute everything would be all right, and the next he'd just blow up for the slightest reason. I'd get such a shock, it'd almost feel like a physical attack. In the end I felt constantly sick with apprehension. It was like I was always on edge, never knowing when the axe was going to fall. It literally felt life-threatening.

Our fear can be a realistic and vital signal about a threat to our well-being or safety. It is important to listen to and act on our valid fears.

Shame

The basic message of abuse is that there is something wrong with us: we are inadequate, unworthy or in some way defective. Most people have the secret fear that they are not good enough as they are. Each humiliating incident of abuse reinforces this fear, and our sense of shame deepens.

> I felt so ashamed that my life had got into such a mess. I'd always seen myself as a strong woman who'd overcome all challenges. Now I was reduced to this frightened, hopeless, tearful creature. Even when Garry was treating me like shit, I wasn't capable of taking a stand against him. I'd rather have died than let other people see me like that. They thought they knew me, but they only knew the strong, competent part of me. Really it was a sham. Underneath I was just this weak, pathetic woman whose life was totally out of control.

Many of us feel terribly ashamed that we cannot get our partner to treat us well. His failure to give us the care and respect we deserve seems to prove we are not worthy of love. We cringe at the thought of other people knowing the mistreatment we put up with, or the lengths to which we go to keep the peace. This increasing shame makes us withdraw from the people around us who could offer support.

Guilt

Guilt is that uncomfortable feeling we get when we believe we have done something wrong. 'Believe' is the operative word here. As women we are constantly given the message that we should be available, caring and unselfishly nurturing to all people, at all times. We should keep our partners satisfied; create happy families; have healthy, well-behaved children; run well-organised homes, and be well groomed and efficient. We should be our partner's workmate, best friend, counsellor, loyal supporter and passionate lover. (See 'To be a woman . . .', p. 84.) Whenever we fall short of these impossible standards, we tend to feel guilty. Controlling men know just how to use this to their own advantage.

> Peter would expect me to be there for him constantly. He often twisted things around to make it seem as if I was being selfish. He'd go round with this long face doing his 'poor me' act, and I'd wind up feeling terribly guilty and give myself a really hard time: 'I should've stayed home last night, I should've cut that phone call short, I should've given him sex this morning.' On and on. I was so hard on myself, it was crazy. I felt so guilty most of the time, I had myself tied up in knots. Often he was the one being mean to me and I was feeling guilty!

Anger

Anger is a healthy response to being humiliated, rejected, put down or violated in any way. In an abusive relationship we often deny ourselves the satisfaction of expressing our outrage. This is partly because we have been taught that 'good' women do not display anger. Good women are 'nice', 'accommodating', 'conciliatory', 'understanding' and 'forgiving'. Angry women are 'bitches' and 'nags'.

We also fear the repercussions of our anger. We know from bitter experience that if we express anger we may provoke our partner's retaliation. Rather than directing our anger at our partner, we often choose the safer option of directing it at ourselves.

> There was no way I was going to get angry with Nigel because I'd come off second best, but I was furious with myself because I didn't have the guts to stand up to him. I told myself that if I was such a coward and a wimp, then I deserved everything that he dished out.

Turning our anger inwards often sends us into helplessness and depression. By numbing our anger we often lose the very part of ourselves which could protect us. (See 'Acknowledge your anger', p. 115.)

Sometimes women do express their anger to their partner, but the social constraints against this mean that they are likely to end up feeling guilty and ashamed. As the woman struggles to stand her ground and fight back, she may even find herself provoked into behaviour that goes against her values.

> I decided I wasn't going to let Phil hit me any more, I was going to defend myself. So I started to hit him back when he hit me. I'd often carry a stick around for protection. This went on until it got to the point where I physically attacked him in town one day in front of other people, and he hadn't even attacked me first. I was so embarrassed and ashamed.

Sadness

As our bright dreams for the future fade, many of us begin to grieve for that loss. Sometimes we know in our heart of hearts that this relationship is not going to survive or that if it does it will never be the way we once believed it would be. Often we grieve for the dying of the relationship long before it actually passes.

I just had this overwhelming sense of sadness all the time. Even when things were going well between us I couldn't shake it off. It was like I couldn't quite believe that the good times were going to last and I was just waiting for the crunch.

Confusion

When our partner denies our reality, twists events and changes the rules, we become confused.

I felt like I was going crazy. Half the time I knew what was happening, but then I'd start to doubt that it was actually as bad as it was. There were times when I'd think, 'I must be over-reacting.' I wanted to believe that it wasn't that bad. At one stage I tried to tell the priest, but he didn't believe me and I became really confused. Was I making these things up about my husband? Why would I lie? Why would I be so emotional?

Our confusion may lead us to fear we are losing our mind. At times, the way we feel and behave seems to confirm this. Many women suffer mood swings, nightmares and panic attacks, and fantasise about suicide or revenge. Although these reactions are frightening, they are understandable responses to our distress. *We are reacting to an unbearably stressful situation, but we are not crazy.*

Questions to consider: Do you feel . . .

- anxious and apprehensive when you hear your partner arriving home?
- intimidated by his manner toward you?
- ashamed to tell other people how you are feeling?
- guilty because you fail to live up to your partner's expectations?
- full of resentment, anger or rage?
- scared that you are going crazy?

The impact on behaviour

In an attempt to combat our partner's increasing control, we change. Many of us wear ourselves to a frazzle trying to keep the peace. We adopt strategies to help us feel more in charge of our situation when in reality we have little control. As we struggle to please, we are doing exactly what our partner intends – and in so doing we sacrifice our integrity and our self-respect. Six strategies many women adopt are: compliance, anticipating their partner's needs, appeasing, seduction, silence and deceit.

Compliance

> I only used to say 'No' on very rare occasions, because if I did Stuart would punish me by not speaking to me for days. I knew I either played it his way, or else. So I went along with just about everything just to keep him happy.

Constantly resisting our partner's control is exhausting. But going along with what he wants often seems to offer an easy way out. Unfortunately, the demands don't stop. Nor does his pressure to capitulate.

Anticipating his needs

> Alan was always losing things and accusing me or the children of touching them. I became very careful to always take note of where he put things. Then if he lost something and got into a temper I could tell him where I saw him leave it. I'd even write notes to remind myself, so if he accused me I could check my notes to see what he'd done with it. It was crazy. I was walking on eggshells.

Gauging other people's moods, reading their behaviour and anticipating their needs is second nature to most women. In the abusive relationship we naturally use these skills to try to stay one step ahead of our partner. While this can be a useful self-protection strategy, it also becomes self-defeating. The more we focus on him, the more we abandon ourselves.

Appeasing

> To try to avoid a blow-up I'd have the children bathed and upstairs out of the way when Frank came home, then they couldn't annoy him. I'd try to make sure that everything he wanted was there so he wouldn't get cross. If he got angry I'd think it was my fault: I wasn't performing efficiently as a wife, mother or housekeeper. If I'd done something differently he wouldn't have lost his temper. Next day I'd try even harder. Now I look back and I know he wanted an outlet for his anger, and no matter what I did he'd have soon found something else to be angry about. I'm surprised I didn't have a nervous breakdown trying to keep two young children quiet and out of the way. It was impossible.

Our partner would have us believe that our shortcomings are the reason for his destructive behaviour. Because we desperately want him to treat us well, we fall into the trap of trying to win his approval. The difficulty is that our efforts are never good enough. He always wants more than we can give. However much we do, there is always something that serves as an excuse for his displeasure. As our increasing efforts meet with less and less success, we become burnt out and empty.

Seduction

> Richard would go into a sulk and I'd really get sick of being shut out. I'd feel so miserable. But if I grovelled for sex it'd get him out of it. I'd have to beg him for it: 'I'm sorry. I love you. Please be nice to me. Please don't do this. You're really making me unhappy.' I didn't really want sex. I just wanted him to talk to me again, instead of treating me and the kids like we were aliens. After sex he'd be fine, until the next thing set him off.

Some of us use sex to gain a reprieve from our partner's hurtful behaviour. We offer sex in the hope that afterwards he will show us the kindness we crave. Sometimes the only affection our partner shows us is during or straight after sex. This time may be the closest we come to feeling loved.

Silence

> I got so tired of James picking up on everything I said and arguing with me that I stopped talking to him unless I had to. But the less I talked, the less I had to say. Over time I lost all my confidence, until in the end we'd go out and I could hardly speak to anyone. I just felt like I had no voice, almost like I wasn't even there.

In the face of hostility many of us choose to suffer in silence. It often seems less risky. If we don't say anything, our words can't be twisted and used as weapons against us; we can't be accused of provoking, nagging, arguing or being wrong. Although silence may offer momentary protection, the cost to self-esteem is high. When we take refuge in silence, we lose a vital part of ourselves.

Deceit

> I didn't know who I was or what I wanted any more. I needed time to think, so I began to pretend that I was going to the gym in the mornings on my way to work. Instead I just sat in the car and wrote about how I was feeling. I was trying desperately to get back in touch with myself. Those times were a real turning point for me. I realised how crushed I was feeling. I didn't feel strong enough to stand up to my partner any more. I knew I needed more support, so I made the decision to get a counsellor and join a local women's group. I decided not to tell Neil about those things either. I couldn't take any more flack. I felt terribly sneaky and guilty in a way, but really it was the best thing I did for myself.

Although it feels uncomfortable to compromise our integrity by telling lies, many of us do it. It is sometimes the only way to gain the privacy, protection or freedom we so desperately need.

Questions to consider: How have you changed? Do you:

- frequently go along with your partner's preferences in the hope of avoiding a blow-up?

- try to anticipate your partner's demands and take care of anything that may upset him?
- use sex to try to get him to treat you better?
- remain silent because you believe that what you say will be distorted, attacked, ignored or criticised?
- lie to your partner to avoid his disapproval or anger?

Having identified the strategies we have used in our attempts to resolve our situation it is important we don't give ourselves a hard time about them. For some women these coping strategies mean survival.

Impact on physical and mental health

The profound effects of domination manifest themselves in a myriad of ways. Masked by our denial, the changes in us often creep in unnoticed. In the midst of our nightmare, we are often in far worse shape than we allow ourselves to know. When we do recognise that our health is deteriorating, we often don't realise it is a result of the way our partner treats us. Instead we see it as further proof of our inadequacies, or even craziness. As we are pushed to the edge of our endurance, many alarming symptoms may appear.

Stress-related illness

I had three totally bald spots on my head from the stress. I lost two and a half stone in two months. I got to the stage I could hardly walk because I had a chronic stomach ulcer. I didn't even realise. The doctor said it had been caused by extreme stress and drinking alcohol on an empty stomach. I had no idea that I was under so much stress, or that it could affect me like that.

Loss of confidence

There was a stage I couldn't even go down to the shop without suffering. It was just awful to go into that shop and to have to speak to the person behind the counter to ask them for whatever I wanted. The whole world

around me was so frightening. I just felt so powerless,
like a nothing. I couldn't relate to anyone.

Sense of split lives

I felt I was living two totally different lives. When I
went to work I'd be really together. People would tell
me their problems and I'd be full of love and give the
impression that everything was fine. Then when I went
home it was like an instant depression came down on
me. I'd go into total silence because of all the aggro and
tension. I was so different; no wonder I thought I was
going nutty.

Spiritual disconnection

As things got worse I prayed and prayed for help. I had
experienced God's love working in my life at other times,
but during this darkest of dark times there seemed to
be no God. I couldn't sense His presence any more, and
there didn't seem to be any evidence of Him in my life.
There was no connection and no help, no matter how
hard I prayed. I was in a hell hole of total despair. I felt
utterly abandoned, betrayed and alone.

Exhaustion

I stayed as long as I could, but eventually I couldn't even
eat. It got to the stage that my body was just shaking
and I didn't have the strength to stand up any longer. I
thought, 'I'll die, and then who will look after the
children?'

Acute emotional pain

I was in constant pain in the end. It felt as if my
heart and gut had been ripped out of me, and there was
a burning ache where they should've been. My
throat felt so blocked I could hardly breathe. It was
excruciating.

Frequent crying

I just couldn't cope with the constant demands and
pressure any more. I was crying all the time. I had a
responsible job and I couldn't afford to go under, but
someone would say, 'Are you all right?' and I'd just burst
into tears. I was so used to being mistreated.

Helpless rage

I just hated him. When he went out I'd stand at
the window and pray that he'd write himself off in
the car because I just didn't want to see him again.
I knew the moment he walked back in the door it
would all start over again and I just couldn't hack it
any more. Inside of me there was a real rage but I didn't
dare show it.

Depression

I sunk really low, although I didn't realise how bad I
was at the time. I used to have this vision of myself at
the bottom of these enormous sand dunes, desperately
struggling to climb up. Every time I managed a step, I
just slid down even further. I was exhausted with the
effort. Nothing I did seemed to be any use any more.
No matter how hard I tried, it was impossible. Life
wasn't worth living. It was misery. I hated it. I wanted
to be out of it so I wouldn't have to feel the pain any
more.

Feeling 'on the edge'

I felt like everything had stopped, and yet everything
was frenetic. I couldn't sit still. I just had to be on the
move all the time. I couldn't eat and went down to seven
and a half stone. I was just a nervous wreck, really strung
out.

Abuse of food, alcohol or drugs

I was so unhappy and miserable that I was heavily into tranquillisers. Eventually I alternated between alcohol, tranquillisers, dope and any other illegal drugs I could buy. I just took everything I could get my hands on. I figured that somewhere along the line something had to make me feel better. But it didn't. It almost killed me.

Desperation to escape

I'd always been too much of a coward to kill myself, but I thought that the only way I'd ever get peace was six feet under with daffodils growing on top. That was my dream of bliss and peace. I was always feeling trapped. I just wanted to get away, and I didn't know how. Then I had a horrendous car accident. It was like it was the only way I could get free. I was actually dead on arrival at the hospital. It was a year before I got out. I had to learn to walk again.

Bizarre behaviour

I stood there banging my head against the wall until it hurt, to see if it was all real. I couldn't believe what was happening. I felt so confused and totally helpless, as if I was going mental. Me, a sensible person with a good job, was reduced to this snivelling wreck, standing there banging my head against the wall in sheer disbelief.

Acute fear and panic

I was in so much absolute fear all the time, I was completely desperate. If I let it overwhelm me, it felt like something physical flowing through me. So I used to hold my stomach muscles tight and try not to let the fear out.

Breakdown

I was driving around one day and all of a sudden I had a blackout and I didn't know where I was, where I had come from, where I was going or why I was in the car. I didn't know anything. I pulled over but I was too scared to get out of the car. I didn't know how to get back home. I had my kids to pick up, but I couldn't think where they were. My brain was obviously overloaded, and it had just shut off. For about an hour I sat there telling myself that if I just relaxed it'd come back to me. I realised that my mind had more or less gone, but I just kept on praying really hard. That was the worst experience of my life. Horrible!

Desire to commit suicide

I came within six inches of walking out in front of a truck. I could have just stepped out and then I'd have been dead and I wouldn't have had to worry about it all any more. But I didn't. I looked at the truck driver's eyes. It was like he knew what I was thinking, and I knew what he was thinking, and I couldn't actually put him in that position. I knew if I was going to kill myself then I had to do it myself. I couldn't involve anyone else in it.

Desire to kill

I was desperate to be free of Kevin. I got my sharpest carving knife and stood over him while he was asleep. At that moment I didn't even see him as a person. He was some kind of evil entity: a cancer that was inside me, devouring me, sucking every breath of life out of me. I visualised dozens of stab wounds in his body, with blood spurting out. The more holes I put in him, the more chance there was that he would die. It seemed like hours I stood there, conscious that if I killed him I might never see my kids again. When I look back on that night I'm still shocked that I reached that point of desperation.

I have never hurt anyone in my life. I can't even bear the sight of blood.

Questions to consider: How is your health affected?

- Do you identify with any of the above symptoms of distress?
- Do you need to seek outside help to deal with any of these symptoms?

If you have identified with some of the women's reactions described here, it is reassuring to see these symptoms for what they are: very real distress signals which need to be taken seriously. (See 'How close to burnout are you?' p. 143).

If you need specialised help to deal with your symptoms, please consult the resource list on pp. 244–58 for contact numbers. There is no shame in seeking help. When we are living in a stressful situation, it is often just too hard to cope alone. For further information on depression, suicidal thoughts, and problems with alcohol or drug abuse, see Chapter 6.

Childhood abuse

Abusive relationships hit us doubly hard if we have been abused as children. It is a harsh and unfair fact that many of us have been. This early abuse undermined our self-esteem, robbed us of a strong self-image and invaded our defences. Our resulting vulnerability can make us easy targets for abusive men.

As children we learned that we had no rights or power. Our voices were not heard, our boundaries were not respected and we were not cherished for being ourselves. We did not receive the unconditional love that we needed to enable us fully to believe in our own worth.

Now we feel the agony of reliving those times. Our shaky beginnings have taught us to doubt our strength, be unsure of our limits and to expect pain to be inflicted by those we love. Our childhood feelings of guilt, shame and helplessness are rekindled. We may feel small and defenceless in the face of our partner's hostility. We may continue to reach out desperately for the love we need to heal our wounds, just as we did when we were children. We may feel terrified of being left without protection, abandoned in a world we believe is harsh and cruel.

As innocent children we did not deserve to be mistreated; nor do we now. Then, we were truly powerless to stop the abuse. Now, as adults, we do have power and choices, yet we often feel unable to acknowledge them. At this time we need our own compassion. When we are feeling at our most helpless, we are reliving our childhood doubts and fears. It is then we need to take the steps necessary to nurture and protect ourselves. (See 'Caring for yourself', p. 111, 'Shield yourself', p. 170 and 'Healing past wounds', p. 213.)

How are you feeling?

Facing the impact of our partner's behaviour can stir up deep feelings. Naming these feelings can help to make them more manageable. What did you feel as you read this chapter? There are numerous possibilities. Here are a few. Which ones do you relate to?

• Relieved	• Overwhelmed	• Anxious
• Numb	• Validated	• Tearful
• Hopeful	• Shocked	• Reassured
• Ashamed	• Comforted	• Afraid
• Sympathetic	• Angry	• Strengthened

Sharing your feelings

Acknowledging our feelings to ourselves is important, but expressing them to others helps to release them. When the burden of our sadness has been heard, a load has been lifted off our shoulders. When we share our deepest shame with someone else, and that person still accepts us, it is enormously affirming. (See 'The importance of feelings', p. 115.)

If possible, seek out a trustworthy person to share your feelings with. Although it is important to get support, choose the person you talk to carefully. An insensitive person can make you feel worse. (See 'Choosing a confidant', p. 97.) If there is no one suitable to share your feelings with at the moment, consider using a counsellor or therapist. For details on how to choose a counsellor see p. 106.

Remember who you are

> *Within each of us there is an innately healthy and intuitive creature, sure of her instincts, passionate about her creative work, gifted as a healer and blessed with an ageless wisdom.*
>
> – from *Women Who Run with the Wolves*,
> Clarissa Pinkola Estes

It is important to clearly identify the destructive impact our partner's behaviour is having on us. However, in acknowledging our diminishing sense of identity, conflicted emotions, adaptive behaviour, and symptoms of distress, it is vital to remember that these things are not who we are. We are much more than this. Regardless of how many mistakes we have made, or how off track our lives have become or how badly we feel about ourselves, there is a part of ourselves that remains pure and intact. It is that essence we need to identify with and believe in, as we begin to reconnect with our inner strength.

Chapter Three

Why Does Our Partner Treat Us This Way?

The big question most of us want answered is: 'Why?' We believe that if we just knew the reasons for our partner's behaviour, we would somehow make sense of our situation. Knowing why would give us the means to make everything all right. Many of us waste years on a fruitless search for a logical explanation.

This chapter examines the beliefs and excuses which are commonly used to explain men's abusive behaviour: alcohol, drugs, anger, his childhood abuse, stress, mental illness and our inadequacy. It also offers a less well-known explanation which is given by many professionals working in the field of woman abuse: he chooses to behave as he does.

'It's because of the alcohol/drugs'

If our partner uses or abuses alcohol or drugs, this can seem like a logical explanation for his destructive behaviour. Alcohol or drug use does not *cause* a man to abuse his partner. Many men who abuse alcohol or drugs *never* abuse their partner, and many men who are not alcohol or drug abusers *do*. In fact, women abuse and alcohol or drug abuse are different problems which need to be addressed separately.

It can be very convenient for our partner to blame his 'loss of control' on alcohol or drugs. By claiming he does not remember his actions when he was 'under the influence', he can completely avoid taking responsibility for his behaviour. But if our partner really believes alcohol is 'causing' him to hurt the ones who love him, why does he choose to continue drinking?

Distressingly, people who work with abusive men report that some of these men acknowledge that when they want to abuse their partner they deliberately drink first, so that they can blame it on the alcohol. Many women state that although their partners started out abusing them only when they were intoxicated, they eventually began to abuse them when sober as well. Women also report that when their partners did give up their 'poison', the abuse did not stop, although sometimes it changed form.

> When he stopped drinking, he stopped hitting me, and when he stopped hitting me I was so grateful. But he was so clever with his words and put-downs, I didn't see that he had even more power over me. In fact I was getting more downtrodden than ever.

Unless sobriety brings with it a willingness to work at the established pattern of control, our partner's abuse will probably continue.

When an abusive man joins a programme to overcome an addiction, his partner is likely to feel she must stay with him to support him. Society expects the woman to 'stand by her man' when he attempts to go straight. However, society is seldom informed about the emotional and physical abuse that the woman endures, often long after her partner has concluded his 'recovery' programme.

'He's got a problem with anger'

It is often assumed that a man's inability to deal appropriately with his anger causes abuse. It is comforting to believe that our partner is out of control and cannot stop himself from hurting us. But there can be a chilling level of control behind the anger. If your partner has a 'problem with anger', consider these questions:

- Does he vent his anger on everyone he comes into contact with, or dump it just on you?
- Does he abuse you in public, or only in private?
- Can he stop short and become a 'good guy' if he is interrupted by other people?

- Is he able to control his anger around people he wants to impress?
- In a rage, does he break his own possessions or yours?
- If he is violent, does he avoid bruising parts of your body that would be visible to others?

Considered actions like those listed above show the control that is often behind our partner's supposedly 'uncontrollable' anger.

If your partner uses the excuse that he has a problem with anger, he could attend a non-violence programme to learn to deal with it. (See the resource list on pages 244–58 for contact phone numbers). If he continues to take his anger out on you, he is actually making a choice. (See 'If your partner is willing to get help', p. 156.)

'He's had a terrible childhood'

While it is true that many controlling men have grown up in abusive homes, others have not. In any case, this is not an excuse for current abuse. Many men from abusive backgrounds make a choice never to inflict that pain on their own families.

We too may have suffered abuse as children, yet this does not give us the right to abuse other people. If we were to abuse our children, it would not be tolerated. Why then should we tolerate our partner's abuse on such grounds? Each of us can choose not to perpetuate what was done to us as children and seek help with this if we need to.

> I found myself in a counselling role with Tim, going back over his life and his formative years, trying to search out where all this began. All the time I was telling myself, 'This man's in a lot of pain and that's what's causing him to act so irrationally.' I excused him and justified what was happening to such an extent that I didn't even believe it myself.

Although we may spend many long hours listening to, supporting and counselling our partner in the hope of helping him resolve his destructive childhood, this usually proves ineffective. Our relationship is not a counsellor–client one. Most of us are not trained in this field, and even if we were, counselling a partner is not appropriate. If our partner is serious about dealing with his past, it is his responsibility to seek professional help from a counsellor or therapist.

'He's under stress'

Stress is a part of most of our lives. In fact it is extremely stressful living with a partner who constantly harasses us. Is our stress any less intense than our partner's? Probably not! Despite our high stress, most of us go to great lengths to create a stress-free home for our partner in the hope of keeping him calm. What does he do to reduce our stress?

> There was always a reason why Ian was stressed out. Sometimes it would be because he was unemployed and he felt lonely staying home all day while I went out to work. Then when he got a job it wouldn't be long before he was stressed out about that too. It took me quite a while to realise these were just excuses for his bad moods. It seemed like whatever stress I was under, it was nothing compared to his.

'Maybe he has a mental illness'

The vast majority of men who abuse are not mentally ill. *Abuse is a learned behavioural choice*, not a mental illness. Sometimes our partner's behaviour seems so irrational that mental illness seems the only possible explanation. But if our partner were abusing us because he was mentally ill, we could expect him to indiscriminately abuse other people as well. Most controlling men save their abuse exclusively for their loved ones.

'It's because of the things I do'

In the absence of other logical explanations, most of us eventually resort to blaming ourselves for causing our partner's abusive behaviour. Our partner tells us that he criticises us because we are inadequate; withdraws because we are demanding; lashes out because we provoke; and is sexually demanding (or rejecting) because we fail to satisfy. As our partner continues to undermine our confidence, we begin to accept his claim that if only we were 'better', everything would be all right.

Adopting the self-blame explanation can give us the thread of hope we're so desperately seeking. If we believe we are in some way responsible for the abuse, then we can believe that we also have some power to prevent it. This comforting illusion can keep us trying to get it 'right' for a long time.

These are just a few of the explanations we may adopt and discard in our search for an answer to our partner's abuse. This search can feed our hope for change and distract us from the reality of our situation for a very long time. In a sense, our search for an answer to the question, 'Why?' is futile. Even if we found the perfect explanation, *we* would still be unable to change the problem. Ultimately, it is up to our partner to decide what he is going to do about his behaviour. *Only he can choose to change.*

You may like to reflect on, or write about, these questions:
- What explanations have you adopted (and perhaps discarded) to explain your partner's behaviour?
- If you stopped looking for a logical explanation, what could you be left with?

A new reason to consider

In our deeper and deeper search for the reason, we often overlook the most obvious yet painful possibility. Perhaps our partner is behaving like this simply because he wants to. If we stop to think about it, controlling men *do* gain a number of advantages from their bad behaviour. Some of their gains may include:
- a position of power in the family;
- a sense of importance;
- the satisfaction of having his own way most of the time;
- a compliant partner who strives to please him;
- plenty of reassurance, attention and special privileges.

Exercise: What does your partner gain?

Think of a time recently when your partner used punishing or intimidatory tactics against you.

Write out your answers to the following questions:

- What happened?
- What did my partner do?
- What did I do, and why?
- What did my partner gain?

For example:

What happened? I told Bob my family were coming over to dinner on Sunday.

What did Bob do? He got angry and shouted insults about my family. Then he stormed off to bed saying I didn't care about his feelings.

What did I do? I felt guilty and ended up apologising and telling him I did care. I agreed not to have my family over on a Sunday again. I tried to make it up to him by cooking him a special meal.

What did he gain?

- He gained the satisfaction of getting his own way.
- He gained my agreement not to invite my family over on Sunday again.
- He got to have me to himself this Sunday.
- He gained an apology.
- He gained my attention and efforts to please him.
- He gained a particularly nice meal.
- He gained my reassurance about how important he is to me.
- He gained the excuse to get angry and make a scene.

When we do this exercise we can usually see quite clearly that our partner does make gains through his controlling behaviour. And the gains are usually made at our expense. It is, however, very distressing to consider that our partner may deliberately hurt us. This possibility goes against everything we have been taught and believe about intimate relationships.

I searched endlessly for a logical explanation for the way
Brian was treating me. I made so many excuses. When
I finally had to accept that he was mistreating me
because he chose to, it almost broke my heart. It just
seemed beyond comprehension. How could he care
more about making me do what he wanted than about
how he was hurting me? Surely he knew that I loved
him, and I'd have done anything to make him happy
anyway?

Although it can hurt to see the truth, when we do see it,
we are in a more powerful position to protect ourselves.

Chapter Four

Seeing the Wider Picture

Most of us live out our relationship struggles privately. No matter how bad things get, we pretend to the outside world that all is well, prevented by shame from confiding in other people about our distress. Caught by the secrecy that surrounds destructive relationships, we have no way of knowing how many other women are also trapped, silent and alone, in similar situations. We also have no way of knowing that our bewildering personal experience is part of a wider picture. While each of our situations is unique, there are strikingly similar patterns of behaviour which run through most accounts of controlling relationships.

Standing back to see our situation in the wider context can be enlightening and empowering. This chapter explores the common threads which are found in controlling relationships. It looks at the way control develops; the cycle of abuse; the attitudes and beliefs about male supremacy that controlling men frequently hold; the ways in which our conditioning as women interacts with this. It also looks at society's role in condoning abuse, and the myths surrounding abusive relationships.

How has this happened?

One of the most difficult aspects of coming to terms with a controlling relationship is the realisation that life with your partner has turned out so differently from what you expected when you decided to share it with him. How did a relationship which once promised so much deteriorate so badly? For many women the pattern is similar.

The heavenly honeymoon

The beginning of the relationship is usually happy and romantic. Many controlling men are particularly charming and entertaining, and appear to be caring, attentive and adoring lovers.

> Don idealised me and put me on a pedestal, as if I was the most marvellous woman in the world. I still remember feeling the responsibility of such adoration. I'd often pinch myself and think, 'My God, here is a man who actually thinks that I'm so clever and educated and intelligent.' He was very affectionate and loving. My best friend. He had an incredibly good sense of humour and was always making me laugh.

Our partner is often so plausible there is no way of knowing that he is anything other than who he seems. He certainly does not seem capable of deliberately hurting us. He is likely to be popular and well thought of by other people, and he may even hold an important position in society.

Warning bells

Looking back, most of us can pinpoint a certain incident with our partner that rang the first warning bells. At the time we had no way of knowing that this was a glimpse of much worse things to come. So we gave our partner the benefit of the doubt, and dismissed his bad behaviour as an out-of-character incident.

> Everything had been going so well. Then we went out for the day with my children and they did something really small that upset him. He got in an absolute fury about it and drove like a maniac all the way home. I was totally terrified, too scared to say one word until we got home, in case he killed us all. Then I told him I didn't want to see him any more because I didn't want to be around that sort of behaviour. For the next five days he sent roses and love notes every day, and I started to think maybe he was sorry for what he'd done. Perhaps I was being over-sensitive. Then he came around and

wanted to take me out to dinner. After we'd been away for a lovely romantic weekend, that was it. I was hooked again.

An escalating nightmare

Most controlling men are careful not to show their true colours until they feel reasonably confident of our on-going commitment. The increase in their control often coincides with events that bind us more closely to them: we begin to live together, marry, become pregnant, give up work or move away from friends and family.

> It wasn't long after Bob moved into the house that he began to police and question everything I did. Soon he was querying every part of my lifestyle and discouraging people from coming to the house. Eventually I realised that Bob was very skilfully getting me more and more to himself. No matter how much of my time I gave him, he wanted more. He started telling people I was not well, implying that I was crazy. He began to get really hostile toward me, and I was frightened. I was also confused, because it seemed the good, honest, wholesome man I deeply respected and loved was just a sham. In the end I felt in my heart he was trying to break me.

At first we may put our partner's need to control down to insecurity, and attempt to reassure him by going along with what he wants. We believe that as he realises the extent of our commitment he will learn to trust us more. In fact the more we give way, the more controlling our partner becomes.

In between abusive episodes there may be wonderful times of happiness and compatibility that remind us of the early days of our relationship. Unfortunately these good times usually become less frequent as the relationship progresses.

The cycle of abuse

Although we may be unaware of it, there is often a cyclic pattern to our partner's behaviour. The three phases of tension-building, explosion and loving reconciliation have been identified as a common pattern which operates in many abusive relationships.[1]

> I didn't realise it for a long time, but there was a definite cycle to Paul's outbursts. Every so often he'd start getting all stressed and hyped-up. He'd come home and start picking on me about the house. It made me really nervy and I'd consciously think, 'I'm not going to react this time,' but then I'd be so anxious I'd end up getting hyped-up too. Then there'd be a major fight. It would start out verbally, but sometimes he'd even end up hitting me. Afterwards all my anger would be gone, and I'd go numb and not really be functioning, and he'd be all lovely and say he was sorry and it wouldn't happen again. Then things seemed to go along quite well and he'd be nice to me until the next blow-up.

This cycle helps to explain why we stay for so long in a destructive relationship. The most likely time for us to decide to leave would be after a blow-up. But when we are hurt and our partner reaches out to give us the comfort and reassurance we crave, it is such a relief that we are easily drawn back into believing that he is truly sorry and that it will never happen again.

Once begun, the frequency and severity of the abuse usually increases. Over time, this three-phase cycle changes: the tension-building phase becomes shorter and more intense, the explosions become more frequent and severe, and the loving reconciliations become shorter and less intense. Eventually the reconciliation stage of the cycle may stop altogether.

What do controlling men have in common?

Controlling men come from every walk of life, race, class and culture. Given their obvious differences, it is remarkable that many of them display very similar patterns of behaviour.

The controlling man usually:

- denies his behaviour is controlling and destructive;
- blames his partner for causing the abusive episodes;

- minimises the effect of his behaviour on his partner;
- refuses to take responsibility for changing his behaviour.
  He may also:
- be highly critical of his partner;
- be excessively jealous;
- present a dual Dr Jekyll and Mr Hyde personality.

Controlling men often hold many similar attitudes and beliefs about their role as men. They usually believe:
- Men are superior to women.
- A man should be the undisputed head of the household.
- Men have the right to dominate and control their partners.
- A man has the right to special privileges in the home.
- A man's demands take priority over children.
- A man has the final say on how joint money is spent.
- A man is entitled to demand access to his partner's body when he chooses.
- A man is entitled to punish his partner if she does not comply with his demands.

Woman abuse in all forms develops from attitudes like these. Sometimes we have no idea that our partner holds these beliefs. We may even think that he is reasonably sympathetic to women's aspirations and interests. But it pays to stop and think, and to consider carefully the differences between what he says in public, and what he says and does in private.

Questions to consider. Does your partner . . .

- regard you as his property, there to meet his needs, with few, if any, rights of your own?
- rule your life and make most of the decisions without taking your opinions into account?
- believe that the house and children are your sole responsibility and refuse to do his share, even if you are sick or employed in full-time work outside the home?
- consider himself a higher priority for your attention than the children?

- refuse to let you work outside the home or allow you to take only the jobs that he approves of?
- demand sex as of right, regardless of your desires or wishes?
- hold negative attitudes about women in general?

The historical context of abuse

To understand where attitudes like these come from, it is necessary to put male and female relationships into their historical context.

For hundreds of years men have legitimately dominated women. Traditionally marriage gave a man licence to control and abuse his wife. The law placed a married woman under the authority of her husband. Marriage deprived her of her legal right to own property, to divorce or to have guardianship over her children. It reduced her to the status of a child. Total surrender and obedience were expected. The husband became the judge of whether she was fulfilling her wifely duties adequately. If he deemed she was not, he had the right to chastise her as he saw fit – including physically.

In the eighteenth century the British common law 'rule of the thumb' restricted a man's right to beat his wife to the use of a whip no thicker than his thumb. The possibility of being beaten with a weapon of this size is horrifying enough, but the interpretation and enforcement of this law left much to be desired, as the British philosopher John Stuart Mill observed in 1869: 'The vilest malefactor has some wretched woman tied to him, against whom he can commit any atrocity except killing her . . . and even that he can do without too much danger of legal penalty.'[2]

Today, assault against a partner is a legally punishable offence. But we need to remember the historical roots from which our present society has grown. Attitudes are passed from one generation to the next; the idea that women are second-class citizens who are there to serve and service men is still deeply embedded in our society.

Physical violence is the ultimate expression of men's dominance over women, but emotional violence is also part of that same power and control continuum. Men are socialised to be competitive and aggressive in pursuing what they want. Individual men's attitudes are a reflection of a society that believes men are more important than women. Societal attitudes to the abuse of women help to keep us suffering in silence. And abuse thrives on secrecy!

Society's role

Almost invariably people respond to hearing about women abuse with questions like, 'What did she do to deserve it?' or 'Why does she put up with it?' These questions imply that the woman is in some way to blame for her own abuse. A more appropriate question to ask is, 'Why does this man choose to abuse his partner?' or 'Why do men choose to abuse women?' But instead of placing the responsibility for his abuse where it belongs – fairly and squarely on the controlling man – society prefers to focus on the woman. His shameful behaviour then becomes our shame.

In fact society can condone and even encourage the continuation of our partner's abuse. This happens when:

- Family and friends ask what we did to deserve the abuse, sing our partner's praises and urge us to stay in the relationship for the sake of the children.
- The church reminds us of the sanctity of marriage, tells us to forgive and forget our partner's abuse, and urges us to try harder to please our man.
- Doctors prescribe tranquillisers to deaden our symptoms of distress, while ignoring the reason for our deteriorating mental health.
- Neighbours turn a blind eye and a deaf ear to domestic violence, believing the abuse of a woman by her partner is private and more acceptable than an attack by a stranger.
- Medical workers treat the injuries inflicted by our partners without probing for details of how we obtained them.
- The media gives a low profile to crimes committed against women by their partners and continues to portray women as sex objects available for men's gratification.

- Counsellors ignore the reality of our partner's abuse, while counselling us to change our behaviour to improve the relationship.
- Police try to resolve situations of family violence by adopting a conciliatory role and viewing both parties as equal, instead of recognising that there is a perpetrator and a victim.
- Judges underestimate our valid fear of our partner and are more concerned with his needs than with our need to be protected.

All of these reactions give the controlling man a very clear message: he has the right to treat us as he does. There are few, if any, consequences for his behaviour.

There are many myths about women abuse. However incorrect, they serve a purpose: they help to keep society feeling safe and complacent. People like to believe that abuse could never happen to them. They prefer to adopt the idea that abuse happens only to 'other' people, those of a different ethnic or socio-economic group, or from a dysfunctional family: that way they can distance themselves. It is safer to 'blame the victim' than to accept that they too could be subject to abuse.

Society's tendency to blame women is reflected in the most common myths surrounding women abuse.

The 'She provoked it' myth

Rather than accepting the unpalatable reality that some men deliberately choose to harm their partners, some people prefer to believe that we 'deserve' to be abused. This preserves their sense of fairness and justice. Because we take so much responsibility for keeping our partner 'happy', many of us get hooked into believing this myth as well. Yet all abused women can remember times when their partner was determined to create an issue about which to abuse them. Provocation never entered into it. Some men have even violently assaulted their partner when she was asleep.

It can be convenient to forget that, regardless of any so-called 'provocation', a man always has the choice to walk away rather than to abuse.

The 'She has a history of abuse that she is replaying' myth

Abuse is rife in our society. Some of us, but certainly not all, have experienced previous abuse. The thing that attracted many of us to our partner in the first place was his apparent kindness and charm. Most of us never dreamed that behind that facade was a man who was capable of inflicting so much pain.

In any case, *our history is not the issue*. Our partner's destructive behaviour is! Even if we did want our partner to abuse us, we could not *make* him do so. That is a choice he makes, and it has nothing to do with our history.

The 'She puts up with it, she must like it' myth.

Society still believes that many women are masochistic; that is, that they enjoy being victimised and hurt.

There are many reasons we stay in abusive relationships for as long as we do (these will be explored in Chapter 5), but enjoyment of pain is not one of them! In fact we usually turn ourselves inside-out to avoid the pain our partner inflicts. Eventually most women in abusive relationships do leave, despite the economic and other disadvantages they face.

It is easy to see why we fall into the trap of blaming ourselves for our partner's abuse. We are doing what society as a whole does.

The labels we are given

If they see we are not coping with our situation, other people often put labels on us. We may be described as 'dysfunctional', 'highly strung', 'hysterical', 'a hypochondriac', or 'neurotic'. These labels define us as having something wrong with us, and yet do not take account of the reasons for our distress. Sometimes these labels are given to us by professionals who fail to probe beneath our symptoms to the underlying issues. The fact that our partner's abuse is causing our distress is overlooked. The implication then becomes that because we are 'sick' we are causing the relationship difficulties. Not only

are labels usually unhelpful, disempowering and demoralising, they often give our partner justification for his
destructive behaviour.

The concepts of co-dependency and 'women who love
too much' can also have a subtle blaming quality. Broadly
speaking, a co-dependent is defined as a person who has
become over-focused on another and driven to meet his needs
while ignoring her own. Women have long been socialised
into putting others first at their own expense, yet the label
'co-dependent' implies that the woman is sick for doing it.

In attempting to overcome our partner's abuse, we will
undoubtedly have become over-focused on him, and it is
healthy to look at changing this, but these changes need to
be addressed in a positive way. Adopting a label that defines
us as sick can add to our feelings of inadequacy, shame and
self-blame. It can also keep us working to change ourselves,
while overlooking just how inappropriate and unacceptable
our partner's behaviour is. In deciding whether to adopt the
co-dependent label and use this approach to work on making
changes in your behaviour the most important consideration
is whether it empowers you and increases your self-esteem.
If it does, go to it!

To be a woman . . .

All of us are influenced to some extent by social expectations.
From birth we are taught what it is to be a woman. We learn
that girls are 'sugar and spice and everything nice'. Boys are
encouraged to master their world through the rough and
tumble of boisterous play, and their sisters are encouraged
to be passive and pretty. Myths and fairy stories like
'Cinderella', 'The Sleeping Beauty' and 'Snow White' give us
the message that a female is dependent on her passive
goodness to obtain the man who will make her life complete.

As we go through life, the media and society constantly
define female identity for us. We are bombarded with
messages telling how to look 'nice', smell 'nice' and be 'nice'.
Our willingness and ability to build positive relationships and
care unselfishly for others is also regarded as central to our

identity as a woman. This is the usual measure of our 'goodness'.

> The whole pattern I was brought up with was Cinderella stuff. My parents had given me this model where Dad was the head of the household and Mum was devoted to him. But the thing was, he was also devoted to her, so he never abused the power she gave him. It was a respectful relationship. I gave all my power to this man because I thought that was what you did with husbands, and I guess he just picked up the ball and ran with it. I'd learned to go out of my way to make other people comfortable, because that was the loving thing to do. I'd also learned that women were there to serve men, not to make nuisances of themselves by making waves. I was always told that I talked too much and was too loud. So when there was a hassle, all my conditioning said, 'Step back. Take stock. How can I make this better?'

As women we are expected to . . .

- be patient, kind, giving, supportive and available at all times to the people around us;
- be aware of, and meet, other people's needs at the expense of our own;
- take responsibility for sustaining relationships and creating happy families;
- cope efficiently and untiringly with all domestic demands;
- work hard to stay youthful and make our appearance fit the current promoted shape and image;
- please our partner and support him in getting ahead in the world;
- be restrained, not too demanding or independent, never angry;
- love our partner enough to heal and transform him into a healthy, happy man;
- stand by our man, especially during the bad times.

For those of us with a controlling, demanding partner, trying to live up to these ideals is a recipe for disaster.

Wayne seemed to need a lot of attention, so I gave it to him. I used to think, 'If I just give enough, Wayne will feel happy and sure of himself, then he'll be able to give back to me.' But it never happened. There was a crash when we had the babies. Everything became my responsibility. Wayne expected me to do it all, and it was my fault if it wasn't done right. He'd constantly say things like, 'Boring! The cooking has gone down hill. The house and garden is a mess.' I really tried. I used to drive myself until I dropped, but there was no help or compromise. I tried everything I could to make him happy, but I'd get so drained, and then he'd be saying, 'Look at you, you're such a mess.' In the end I couldn't give any more. I just couldn't. I had nothing left.

Women's responsibility for relationships

Relationships are generally seen as women's work. It is usually women who maintain links with family and friends, remember birthdays, buy gifts and arrange social gatherings for both their own and their partner's families. The task of caring for the young, sick and aging members of both extended families often falls to the woman as well.

It is usually the woman who is the communicator, emotional risk-taker, nurturer and peacemaker in an intimate relationship. Taking responsibility for the emotional life of the relationship comes easily to most of us. We have been conditioned into this role since birth. We are automatically tuned into the emotional world of our partner and have developed the ability to understand his inner life far better than he probably does himself. We have become experts at analysing, interpreting and understanding his feelings, but often at the expense of our own self-knowledge and care.

Because we are seen as primarily responsible for building a successful relationship, we automatically feel responsible for a failing one. When things go wrong, we unthinkingly work harder to make them right, while overlooking our partner's role in creating the problems.

The 'miracle' of love?

One of the strongest messages we receive from religion, books, movies and song is that love has the power to work miracles. We are taught that although 'true love never runs smooth', it will triumph over adversity in the end.

We have all heard the saying that 'behind every successful man is a good woman'. The popular theme in books and movies of the untamed man who is transformed by the love of a 'good' woman is present in endless variations. The message is: it is possible to love our discontented, angry, alcoholic and abusive partners 'better'. It is this belief that often keeps us striving to make our relationships work long after they have ceased to be viable.

Many of us see our partner as an unhappy man, wounded by his childhood and driven by his own inner demons. So we reach out with compassion to reassure and comfort, believing that our love has power to heal and help him to grow toward his potential. When he lashes out we excuse him, because we believe he is acting out of his inner pain.

> Keith had had the most dreadful childhood, and he seemed so hurt and battered by life, that my heart just went out to him. I really thought that I could love him better. Even when he was being really nasty to me I felt like I could see beyond all that to the hurt child. I really believed that if I just loved him enough he would come to believe in himself and let that love in. Then he would realise that it was safe to love and he'd stop pushing me away.

Ironically, the more destructive our partner becomes, the more 'lost' we can perceive him to be and the more difficult it may be to leave him. Many of us promised to love 'for better or for worse'. It is not easy to turn away from a man whom we perceive as needing us. But the best way to help our partner face his problems is to take care of ourselves.

> I used to think that Bob behaved like that because he was sick and couldn't help it. I thought he needed me and I was helping him. I realise now that by putting up

with his hurtful and humiliating demands, I was not helping him. No one needs someone to abuse.

Questions to consider

- How strong is your commitment to yourself compared with your commitment to your partner? Do you see your needs as: just as important, more important or less important than his?
- How much of the work of relating do you do, compared to your partner? What percentage of the giving are you doing?
- What beliefs do you hold about the 'miracle of love'? Are you reaching out to your partner in an attempt to heal him?

This chapter has offered some insight into the social factors behind controlling relationships. While we are trapped in self-blame, lost in the search for rational explanations for our partner's irrational behaviour, we remain helpless and bewildered. We gain new clarity only when we stand back and view our situation from a different perspective.

Many of the expectations imposed on us by society, and adopted by us as an important part of our identity as women, are the very things that help us to remain powerless and confused in an abusive relationship. It is reassuring to realise that those of us who find ourselves in abusive relationships started out behaving in similar ways to most other women. The difference in outcome is not because of the way we are, as society would like to believe. It is in the way our partner has chosen to dominate us and exploit our love.

References
1.   Walker, Lenore, *The Battered Woman*. Harper and Row, New York, 1979.
2.   Mill, John Stuart, *The Subjection of Women*, MIT Press, Cambridge, Massachusetts, 1970.

Chapter Five

What Stops Us From Leaving?

If people know about our unhappy relationship they often wonder why we don't leave. We know it is not easy. Our love, hope, fear and sense of responsibility interweave to create a complex range of reasons to stay.

> I just loved him so much. Sure he was hurting me, but there were also wonderful times when we would be close and loving. He could be such fun and make me feel so special. That's very hard to give up. Really, breaking up was the last thing I wanted. All I wanted was for his abuse to stop.

> Despite Geoff's angry nature, he's an okay guy. As his mother was so quick to point out, he's been the epitome of a good husband. He's never been out of work, never gambled, never womanised or been a drunkard. I used to wish he'd beat me up, because then I'd have a reason to leave. That was the only way I could have justified leaving, because he is the father of my children.

> I found it so hard to pull away, because just when I'd think I couldn't stand it any more he'd stop being mean to me and become that wonderful man I had fallen in love with again. It only took a few crumbs of kindness to hook me back into thinking there was hope. I kept believing that if I just hung in there he'd go back to treating me the way he had in the beginning. There'd be nine bad times and one good time, and I'd focus on the good time and pretend the other times hadn't happened or that they weren't that bad. I just didn't want to face the truth that it had all been an act and he

didn't really care that much about me after all. Accepting that was more than I could bear.

I'd always had a conviction that this relationship was meant to be. It was almost like I recognised Dave the first time I saw him, and I just knew we had a future together. It was this conviction that I held on to through thick and thin. I just kept believing that if it was meant to be, then there was going to be some kind of miracle to make things right.

I knew John cared about me and needed me, and I used to think that was holding me in there. That he'd get upset if I left. But I've realised since it was my terror that was holding me back. My terror of coping in the big world alone. I was brought up on stories that you need a man to take care of you. And my friends used to say, 'You've got such a good husband', and that just reinforced my belief that I really should stay put, because he was better than most.

My grandmother, who I was close to, used to say, 'You've made your bed, you lie in it', and really and truly that was repeated to me so much I firmly believed it. I used to think, 'Oh God, that's it. I have to put up with all this for ever.'

I became so depressed I just didn't have the energy to leave him. In the end I'd lost so much confidence that I couldn't relate to anyone. Then I was so dependent on him, and the more he rejected me the harder I clung to him. In the end I literally felt like a drowning person, clinging hold of a liferaft. It seemed like he was all I had, and I was sure I couldn't make it without him.

As a Christian I really did believe that marriage was a commitment, and that you stayed in it and you worked at it. My philosophy was that marriage was for once, and for ever, and that was it.

I just didn't want to give up. I was married to this person, and come hell or high water I was determined to make it work. For a long time I never actually stopped to think what the situation was doing to me.

I didn't want my children to become statistics and to have to go through all the hurt of a separation. I thought it just wouldn't be fair to them.

I was scared of what Chris would do if I left. I worried about how I could hide away from him. Could I get custody of my children, and how was I going to look after them without depriving them in any way? It was hard enough now, going to work and paying a babysitter. I thought it wasn't fair to the children to change their lives that drastically. Now I see that love, and the lack of abuse, would have been enough. The material things didn't matter that much.

I really wanted to believe that we were going to be together for ever. I can still remember sitting out on the deck of our new home watching the sun going down and saying, 'Choice! We've finally got our house and we'll still be sitting here when we're seventy looking at the sunset.'

Even though I knew I should go, I just kept putting it off. Every time I planned to leave, someone's birthday was coming up, or it was nearly Christmas, or I was sick, or the children were unsettled, or I had no one to help me move, or I was too busy at work, or we had a wedding to go to, or I'd invited his parents to stay. And so it went on and on.

I knew I was on my own if I left, because no one believed that John wasn't the nice guy he pretended to be. He'd convinced everyone that I was the one who was totally at fault, that I was the witch and he was so good.

For a long time I just kept hoping that the day would come when Paul would come to his senses and realise just how much I meant to him. I just wanted him to put his arms around me, and tell me he was sorry and promise not to hurt me any more. That would have made it all worthwhile. After all I had given, I just couldn't bear to walk away with nothing.

I stayed so long because I didn't want to cope with any more pain. Having lost my first husband, I knew what grief was like, and I just felt I wasn't ready to take that dive down into the pits. I thought I could cope with staying better than I could the pain of the break-up. Yet really life was nothing, and I was getting worse and worse in myself.

I didn't want to be on my own with two young children. At least I had his financial support and a house to live in and he'd look after the kids from time to time. I had no confidence in my ability to cope on my own.

I was ashamed. I didn't want other people to know my marriage was a failure. I knew that I'd made the mistake everyone had thought I was going to make. I didn't want to shatter the mask I wore outside the marriage of being this super-confident businesswoman. I felt like such a failure.

Given the numerous reasons we have for not leaving, it is hardly surprising that some of us stay far too long. But love and hope do not die the instant our partner begins to abuse us. They die slowly and painfully, as disillusionment and resentment grow. Then fear gradually creeps in. As our confidence becomes battered and our emotional and physical resources dwindle, we often begin to doubt our ability to survive alone and become increasingly immobilised.

Exercise: Clarify your own reasons for staying

When we are clear about our reasons for choosing to stay, it can help us to feel stronger and more in control of our situation. Which of the following reasons do you relate to?

- I still love my partner.
- This is a bad patch, but I believe it won't last.
- The good times are worth the heartache of the bad.
- I'm hoping my partner's behaviour will improve.

- I believe the good in my partner will triumph over the bad.
- My partner has promised not to hurt me again.
- He has promised to get help.
- He is going to counselling (or attending a programme) and is making positive changes.
- I don't want to break my marriage vows.
- Leaving is against my religious/cultural beliefs.
- I believe that if I can just please my partner he will treat me better.
- I am determined to keep trying to make it work until I have done everything that is humanly possible.
- I have invested so much, I can't bear to give up.
- I'm so depressed I haven't got the energy to leave.
- I need my partner. I feel so broken I don't think I can make it alone.
- I'm afraid the stress of leaving might push me over the edge.
- I'm terrified of being on my own.
- I'm afraid I will never be loved again.
- I can't abandon my partner. He needs me.
- I feel sorry for him and believe I can help him.
- He might kill himself if I leave.
- I haven't got the right to deprive my partner of his children.
- It is not fair to deprive the children of the benefits of having two parents.
- I don't like the thought of being 'single' or a 'solo parent'.
- I don't want to have to cope with bringing up the children on my own.
- I'm afraid my partner will get custody of the children.
- I'm afraid for my safety if I try to leave.
- I don't want to give up my financial security.
- I have nowhere to go.
- I'm ashamed to admit I have failed.
- My partner is so charming, other people will think it's all my fault.
- I intend to leave but the time is not right.

Having identified your reasons for staying, consider the following question.

On what are your reasons for staying based? Are they based mainly on:

- your hope for improvement in the relationship;
- your fears about leaving;
- specific problems that need to be overcome; or
- something else?

If you still feel hopeful about your relationship, you will find suggestions for reclaiming your equality within it in Chapter 10. Before endeavouring to make changes within the relationship it is important to get support in your life and build up your self-esteem and sense of inner strength. The next two chapters will guide you in this.

If you are staying in your relationship because you are afraid, it can be helpful to clarify your fears and begin to work on them. (See 'Acknowledging and redefining your fears', p. 177.) Gathering information, enlisting other people's support and ensuring your safety can help to reduce your fears. Many of the practical problems of leaving will be discussed in Chapter 11 (in particular, see 'Tackling problems', p. 178). For suggestions on how to weigh up your concerns and reach a decision, see Chapter 9.

Thinking about leaving can be very emotional, and this chapter may have stirred up some deep feelings. Writing about your feelings can help to release them. (See 'The release of writing', p. 124.) Writing can also be a powerful way of exploring in more depth what is preventing you from leaving.

Chapter Six

Reaching Out for the Support You Need

We are part of the circle . . . when we do what we're afraid to do . . . we are not separate. We are of the world and of each other.

– from *Dreaming the Dark*, Starhawk

As we have seen, living in a destructive relationship eventually wears down even the strongest woman. For some of us, it becomes a matter of sheer survival. Others appear to cope better but still feel increasingly trapped and empty. In this situation it is essential to maintain contact with people who treat us with respect, and to reach out to those who can offer us vital support.

This chapter will explore some of the various options for support: friends and family, support groups and counsellors. It will also help you to take stock of the ways you may be hurting yourself and whether you may be depressed. Information on depression, medication and dealing with an alcohol or drug problem is provided.

Stay connected to people who care about you

In a controlling relationship, our partner's demands, and our own shame and low energy, often separate us from the people who care about us. Contact with these people can be as vital as a heartbeat. We need them to love and support us, hear and validate us, and to remind us of who we really are. They also link us to the freedom of the outside world when the oppression of our own world threatens to engulf us. They are our greatest lifeline.

In our isolation it is easy to imagine that no one cares about us. But people are usually willing to offer support if only they knew we needed it. To remind you of the possibilities for support in your life, try the following exercise.

Exercise: Increase your support

Write a list of everyone you could spend positive time with or could turn to for support if you really had to. These people might include friends, family, work colleagues, your counsellor, support group members, clergy, and acquaintances who may have been through a similar experience to you. Even if you think you are unlikely to call on them, include them on your list, as it is reassuring to have a number of names to choose from.

When you have named all possibilities, choose the two or three people you feel most comfortable with, and make a point of contacting them as soon as possible, whether you intend to tell them about your situation, or just spend time with them.

Confide in others

Many of us keep our distress a closely guarded secret. Silence seems to offer protection against others' disbelief or blame. Although it can be a risk, sharing our story with a supportive person is often the most empowering step we can take. It enables us to feel less alone and gives us a new perspective on our situation. This begins to break our partner's hold over us.

We may think we are betraying our partner by telling others the truth about his actions, but when our partner's behaviour becomes destructive we no longer owe him our silence. Our first loyalty must be to ourselves. Gaining personal support is part of that.

Exercise: Choosing a confidant

If you have not told anyone about your situation before, consider the following questions:

- What are my reasons for keeping silent?
- What am I gaining by my silence?
- What could I gain if I talked to others?
- Is it worth taking the risk?

When you decide to share your difficulties, it is very important to choose a confidant carefully. It pays to be discriminating. Telling the right person is an enormous relief, but telling the wrong person can be devastating if you are met with insensitivity or judgement. When considering confiding in a person, it can be helpful to ask yourself the following questions:

- Do I trust this person?
- Has she or he been supportive and reliable in the past?
- Will this person believe me and be capable of understanding my situation?
- Will this person respect my confidence? Could her or his loyalty to my partner result in my confidence being broken?
- Will this person support me in finding my own answers or will she or he try to take over my life?
- What is my 'gut feeling' about talking to this person?

Before you take the risk of opening up to someone, it is a good idea to set the scene the way you want it. Gain an assurance of confidentiality and let the person know specifically what you need from them: a listening ear, reassurance, opinions or ideas, practical assistance, a shoulder to cry on, whatever. This makes it easier for the listener as well as yourself.

If you have the misfortune to have a negative experience when you confide, don't let that put you off. If your first choice of confidant was not capable of respecting and supporting you, that is a reflection on them, not you. Don't let this stop you gaining the support you need. Try someone else.

Even if you have support people in your life, it is often a good idea to talk to someone at a women's refuge or to someone from social services or a counsellor as well. These people should be skilled at dealing impartially with situations such as yours. (See 'The role of Women's Aid', p. 183 and the Resource List, pp. 244–58.)

Moving out of isolation

Constant conflict often grinds us down to the point where we lose sight of the choices we can make to improve our lives. Our 'peace at any price' approach locks us into a cycle of powerlessness. It is tempting to close off from others when under stress, but the more isolated we become, the more power our partner gains.

Positive involvement outside the confines of the relationship is a real morale-booster. Joining a support group, attending courses, playing a sport, developing a hobby or gaining employment are all possibilities. Any activity that provides a sense of belonging and increases our self-worth is invaluable. And from one decision to do something different can flow far-reaching changes, as these three women's experiences show.

> I didn't want to be a marshmallow and just capitulate any more. I wanted some sort of control back in my life. I knew it was up to me to do it for myself, and I decided to train in office administration so I would have a way of earning my own living in the future. It wasn't easy at the time. When I was doing the course Keith would come home late and hide the car keys to try to stop me from going, but I stuck to my guns. Eventually that training led on to a really secure job.

> I decided to join the kindergarten committee. It was the best thing I ever did. You get really close to people, working together for a common cause. I loved it. I became known as a capable person doing a good job – totally different from the message I got at home. When I saw the support other women had from their partners, it really made me stop and think. I had none of that.

But gradually I gained the confidence to come out from under Craig's shadow. Then someone on the committee offered me a job doing the books in his small company. From there I went on to become the office manager and company secretary and eventually gained a qualification.

I'd had a couple of breakdowns so I decided I had to do something for myself, and I took up yoga. Through that I gradually built up some sort of strength and regained my confidence. Using my sheer will to do strenuous things with my body gave me a sense of power over myself which seemed to extend into other areas of my life. Then when I read the philosophy behind it, that fed my mind as well and made a really big change. I think if I hadn't gone to yoga I'd still be trapped in the same situation now.

It can be a struggle to gain the freedom needed to pursue outside interests. Most controlling men resist their partner's attempts to broaden her horizons, as this threatens their control. You will need to decide if you have the strength right now to cope with this, and whether it is safe to force the issue. If it is possible to hold out for what you want, it is well worth it. (See 'Taking a Stand', p. 163.)

It is difficult to make any kind of change if you are feeling demoralised. Working through a plan of action first helps. The following exercise will guide you in doing this.

Exercise: Taking a positive step

Write down on a sheet of paper one thing you can do to improve your life. You may decide to start with something small which you feel confident you can achieve, or you may choose an important issue that is more challenging but will create a big change. Then write the answers to the following questions:

- What steps do I need to take to achieve this change?
- What is the first step?
- When will I take that step?
- What steps will I take after that?

• If my partner tries to stop me, how will I overcome this?

You will need to muster all your determination to achieve your goal. It is important to anticipate your partner's resistance and have strategies in place that will allow you to proceed with your plan.

Joining a support group

Many women find joining a support group a wonderful lifeline that provides them with the affirmation and sense of belonging they need. In many areas there are groups available for women who are living in abusive relationships, or who are recovering from this. These groups provide support and information, and the added comfort of being with other women who are facing similar difficulties in their lives.

Some women who have an alcoholic partner find joining an Alcoholics Anonymous Al-Anon group useful. These groups offer support to the partners, family and friends of the alcoholic. The participants share experience, strengths and hope in order to solve their common problems.

> Al-Anon made me realise that I couldn't control what my partner did because I had no power over anyone else, only myself. Once I stopped trying to manage my partner's uncontrollable behaviour, I could then put the focus on my behaviour, my insecurities and low self-esteem. Once I was able to look at things in a more detached way, I could begin to separate problems and put what belonged to him on to him and take responsibility for what belonged to me. Realising I didn't have to accept his behaviour got me out of the victim role. The 12-step programme helped me to stop blaming myself, develop my spirituality and my sense of self, and allowed me to deal with the issues from my childhood. It's made me realise how important I am as an individual, and it's given me incredible support, wonderful friendships, a sense of belonging, and a much healthier and more positive attitude.

Acknowledge the ways you are hurting yourself

Attempts to cope with our situation may drive many of us into self-defeating or self-destructive behaviours. There are countless ways we may do this, including:

- giving up the friends and interests that nourish us in order to please our partner;
- blaming and berating ourselves for our partner's abuse;
- attempting to win our partner's approval by behaviour which causes us to lose self-respect, such as pleading, appeasing or seducing;
- using drugs, excessive food or alcohol to numb our pain;
- taking tranquillisers for a long period without addressing the underlying problems.

We can be drawn into these behaviours because they seem to provide immediate relief from our difficulties. But such 'solutions' often end up making us feel even more out of control and worthless.

Exercise: Name your self-defeating behaviours

Make a list of all the things you are doing that add to your distress. Choose one you would like to change, and apply the following questions to it.

- What am I gaining by this behaviour?
- What is it costing me?
- What do I imagine would happen if I were to stop this behaviour?
- How would I cope with that?
- Do I need outside support to help me to make this change?

The support you decide to seek will obviously depend on the issue you are tackling. (See p. 244 for community resources that may help.)

If you have a problem with alcohol or drugs . . .

Women living in abusive relationships are particularly vulnerable to alcohol or drug addictions. Alcohol, tranquillisers or narcotic drugs offer a way to dull our pain, but when we become dependent on them they create many more problems for us.

Addiction adds to our feelings of worthlessness and hopelessness. It also keeps us in a fog that prevents us from thinking clearly or taking action. No one wants to admit to an addiction problem, but denial stops us from seeking the help we need. If you suspect you may be becoming dependent on alcohol or drugs, it is important to seek help.

Some areas have alcohol and drug treatment centres which offer information, support and counselling to help you to break your dependency. Joining a group such as Alcoholics Anonymous (AA) can also be enormously beneficial. Their programmes can offer acceptance and support while you recover from your addiction.

Dealing with depression

As we suppress our feelings, silence ourselves and struggle to cope with the relentless strain of our situation, many of us become deeply depressed. Depression can lead to on-going feelings of intense sadness, isolation, hopelessness and help-lessness. We may feel anxious, agitated and unable to slow down. Alternatively, we may become lethargic and our mood may drop to a deadening flatness. Our feelings may wane, until eventually we experience an absence of any emotion, except possibly pain. We may be preoccupied with morbid thoughts and obsessional worry, and filled with guilt and self-loathing. Our concentration is poor, our motivation low and our outlook bleak. We have trouble remembering how it felt to be happy, and may not be able to imagine feeling happy again.

Are you depressed?

Depression can descend so gradually that we are unaware of the ways it is affecting our thoughts, behaviour and energy levels. Consider the following questions:

- Do you identify with any of the symptoms described above?

- Have you lost interest in the people and activities that previously gave you pleasure?
- Is it an effort to complete normal tasks?
- Are you having trouble getting to sleep, experiencing broken sleep, waking early or sleeping excessively?
- Have your feelings of depression been on-going for two weeks or more?
- Do you feel so hopeless that you believe that nothing would help you?
- Have you considered killing yourself?

If you answered 'yes' to most of these questions, it is likely you are depressed. Suffering depression can be a debilitating and frightening experience, and our fear is often compounded because it doesn't occur to us we are depressed. Instead we believe our intense sensitivity or uncontrollable feelings of panic are proof that we are going crazy. This is not so. Depression is a shut-down that often occurs when our stress has become too great.

Are you feeling suicidal?

Sometimes when we feel desperate and trapped, suicide can seem like the only way out. Depression can trick us into believing that our situation is hopeless and our pain will go on for ever.

> I didn't have the strength to get my life together any more. I thought killing myself was the only answer. It seemed like the only power I had left, and I thought it would make my husband sorry. I never told anyone how bad I was feeling for a long time because I didn't want them to try and stop me. That was a bad mistake, because I'd totally lost my objectivity about what was happening and I'd got dangerously low. Then one day I broke down and told a friend what I was planning. She was so upset that I hadn't told her how bad I was feeling sooner. I can still remember how surprised I was that she cared so much. I'd convinced myself that I wouldn't be any loss to anyone anyway.

You may not believe it at the moment, but your survival

is of the utmost importance. If you are feeling suicidal, it is vital that you get help right away. Phone a friend, counsellor or crisis phoneline and let them know you need help. (See pp. 244–58 for contact numbers.) Make an agreement with friends that you will phone them whenever you feel desperate, *before taking any action to harm yourself.*

Whatever you do, don't act on your suicidal feelings. Your partner has harmed you enough. Don't let him completely destroy you. Remember, depression makes your situation seem more hopeless than it really is. This terrible time will not last for ever. As your depressed feelings lift, you will begin to believe that your life is worth living again. Meanwhile you can ride out these feelings by living one day, one hour or, if necessary, one minute at a time. This dark time will eventually pass, as many of us can testify.

What you can do about depression

It is important to remember that depression is a *temporary* state of mind which has been brought on by the strain of your situation. It is nothing to be ashamed of. People usually make a recovery remarkably quickly once depression has been identified and appropriately dealt with.

For many of us the quickest way to recover from depression is to leave the relationship. However, we may not be prepared to do this. Even if we are, the reality of leaving is often complicated by the loss of confidence, motivation and hope for the future, which are part of the depression. Counselling can help you to work through your feelings and to explore your options. It may also be worthwhile to visit your doctor. She or he can eliminate possible physical reasons for your symptoms and establish whether medication would be helpful (see below for further details).

There are also ways you can help yourself recover from depression. All the suggestions in this chapter and the next are good tools. In particular, it is important to find someone supportive to confide in. Getting in touch with the anger that is hidden under your depression not only helps you clarify the reason behind your depression but can also have the surprising effect of lifting your mood. Exercise is also especially beneficial.

The possibility of medication

There can be times when our mood has sunk so low we do not have the resources to pull ourselves up again, even with help and support. It is then that medication can be helpful. Severe depression creates chemical changes in the body, and medication can help to correct this. There are two types of medication commonly prescribed: minor tranquillisers and anti-depressants. Both treat the symptoms of depression.

Tranquillisers are usually prescribed to control anxiety. Because the body soon begins to tolerate these drugs, an increasing dose must be taken to achieve the same level of calm. Tranquillisers are addictive and should be taken only under careful medical supervision and for a very short time.

Anti-depressants treat the depression by elevating the mood. It may be two or three weeks before they bring about an improvement. There may be some side-effects such as slight drowsiness and a dry mouth; occasionally they also cause constipation and blurred vision. Anti-depressants are not physically addictive but some people can become psychologically addicted, believing their well-being is dependent on the drugs.

The concern in taking medication is that it can relieve the symptoms which are warning us how destructive our situation is. Some women waste years of their life taking medication which anaesthetises them enough to allow them to go on functioning at a day-to-day survival level without making any changes. Taking a course of anti-depressants may lift you temporarily out of the dark hole of depression, but it is important to use that time to obtain counselling and do some honest soul-searching. If no changes are made, then the depression will probably recur when the medication is stopped.

If your doctor recommends medication, find out what the medication will do for you, what effect it will have on your moods, what side-effects you are likely to experience and how long you can expect to take it for. Your doctor is the expert on the medication, but you are the expert on your body. You should both be working together to achieve your good health. Coming off medication should be done with medical supervision.

Counselling help

Going to a good counsellor or therapist can be an excellent way of gaining insight into your situation and achieving the support you need to make changes.

> When I was in a total mess I finally went to a counsellor. She listened to me rave on and cry for about an hour and then she said, 'Is this how someone who says he loves you should treat you?' I suddenly thought, 'No, I don't deserve this.' She pointed out that if every onslaught of emotional abuse had been a physical thump, I would be black and blue all over. Instead, my very real wounds were on the inside where no one could see them. She helped me to see what I had been reduced to – no job, unable to work because my health was packing up, and barely able to look after myself or my children any more.

It is important to choose your counsellor carefully. Some are not knowledgeable about the dynamics of abuse, and their approach can leave you feeling even more self-blaming, confused and immobilised.

When selecting a counsellor or therapist, the most important guide is your own intuition. You need to feel comfortable with that person and believe you can trust them. Ask friends, acquaintances, or your doctor or local women's refuge for recommendations. (Also see the list of resources, pp. 244–58.) When you make the initial contact, ask the counsellor about her or his qualifications and training. You could also explain that you are in an abusive relationship, and ask what experience she or he has had in working with women in similar situations. The following guidelines will help your selection process.

Consider a counsellor who:

- enables you to feel heard, supported, respected and affirmed as a worthwhile person;
- recognises that the issues in the relationship are primarily those of power and control;
- realises you are dealing with a partner whose behaviour is not rational, and with whom negotiation is probably not possible;
- understands and acknowledges the impact the abuse is having on you;
- clarifies your situation, helps you discover and weigh up your options, and supports you in making your own choices;
- helps you to assess your safety and, if necessary, assists you in working out a plan of action for your protection;
- is able to provide you with information on court orders, family law and community resources, including a safe place to go;
- is committed to empowering you to regain control over your life.

Beware of a counsellor who:

- ignores, minimises, defends or condones your partner's bad behaviour toward you;
- seems unable to recognise your feelings of fear, frustration or helplessness about the abuse;
- tries to make you responsible for the abuse by implying or saying that you provoked it or that your 'approach was wrong';
- claims you can prevent the abuse by changing your behaviour;
- encourages you to try harder to please, understand, endure, or forgive your partner's abusive behaviour;
- comes on strong with advice, or gives any kind of ultimatum to force you into a decision you are not ready to make.
- has sexist attitudes: believes the man is the head of the house and the woman's role is to be subordinate to him.

Before beginning counselling, it is a good idea to decide what you would like to gain from it. You probably hope to find ways to make the relationship work, but as you have no control over your partner's behaviour it is important that your goal primarily reflects your own well-being.

Attending counselling may have its challenging and painful moments, but overall it should help you to feel cared about and validated as a person. If this is not happening, you do not have the right counsellor. It is a good idea to evaluate the counselling after five or six sessions. You can do this by using the lists above as a guide. If you are not satisfied, don't be afraid to change counsellors. You are the one in charge, and you have the right to good service.

Spirituality can bring strength

For many women the greatest source of support and comfort is their spirituality.

> Even though I had no one to help me when I was in trouble, I never felt that I was alone. I had this spiritual presence and it helped me to feel strong. When things were really bad and I was desperate and I couldn't even think straight, I'd say, 'My life's a mess. Show me the way.' Then my mind would wander into this spiritual place and I'd suddenly get a very peaceful and relaxed feeling. Things would come into my mind like, 'It's okay. Just relax. You'll make it.' It was like voices were coming into me to guide me, but I didn't feel as though I was thinking.

Spirituality means different things to different people. We may seek and find our spirituality through prayer, meditation, women's spirituality groups, traditional religion, appreciation of nature or staying connected to the part of ourselves that is whole and strong. Although for some women living with abuse creates a spiritual crisis of disconnection, for others spirituality is a major lifeline. In our darkest times, our spirituality can become the one tiny thread we hold on to. The belief that there is something beyond ourselves which can guide us through our pain to safety and peace can keep us from going over the edge.

Chapter Seven

Reconnecting With Your Self

Even the most repressed woman has a secret life, with secret thoughts and secret feelings, which are lush and wild, that is, natural.

– from *Women Who Run With the Wolves*,
Clarissa Pinkola Estes

Our partner's abuse undermines the most precious relationship that any of us has: our relationship with our self. To reclaim that relationship we need to focus on our own feelings, needs and desires before our partner's. We need to put ourselves in the centre of our own life, and become the most important person in our world. We need to rediscover our own power, passion and truth. Instead of trying to discern what is going on in our partner's head and heart, we need to listen to our own yearnings and inner wisdom. Rather than working to earn our partner's occasional, grudging approval, we need to give ourselves the appreciation and love we crave. We need to feed our own hungry heart.

Abuse robs us of our personal power. We also give our power away when we unthinkingly pour more and more of ourselves into a relationship that doesn't nourish and nurture us. Our personal power is depleted when we:

- give ourselves to a partner who doesn't value that gift;
- love that partner more than we love ourselves;
- continue to reach out in the face of rejection and criticism;
- constantly sacrifice our own needs to meet our partner's demands;
- remain silent when we have something we need to say;

- blame, criticise and condemn ourselves;
- deny our desires, needs, feelings and truth, even to ourselves.

The way to reclaim our personal power is to build an honest relationship with ourselves so that we understand, accept and honour our feelings and truth. It may be a slow process, but every time we speak or act in a way that reflects our own truth, we gain back a little of ourselves. As we make choices that support our well-being and protection, we begin to believe in our ability to survive, no matter what.

This chapter will guide you in reclaiming and building your relationship with your self, by accepting and caring for yourself and gaining an awareness of your feelings, thoughts, inner dialogue and self-image. It will also offer suggestions for positive changes you can make in these areas, and explore the benefits of expression through writing.

The power of self-acceptance

The most empowering gift we can give ourselves is the gift of self-acceptance. When we are not able to deal with our situation as we would like to, many of us grow to despise ourselves. Sometimes our expectations about what we can do to confront our situation are quite unrealistic.

> I felt so furious at myself because I was too afraid to move or retaliate, to say, 'Stuff you. Who the hell do you think you are? You've got no right to talk to me like this.' I couldn't, because I was too fearful of my world crashing in on me, fearful that he'd be so angry with me for daring to say that, that he'd kill me.

When our partner attacks us for not measuring up to his standards, we often accept his judgement and join him in berating ourselves. We also get hooked into trying to prove we are 'good enough', while secretly fearing we may not be. Imagine how different it would be if we refused to accept our partner's judgement as the measure of our worth; if, instead, we allowed ourselves to believe that despite our short-comings, we were okay. Our partner would have lost much of his power to manipulate and hurt us.

When we stop believing in our own worth, we are defenceless. To re-establish a sense of self-worth, we need to make a conscious commitment to accept ourselves exactly as we are. When we are real with ourselves and accept all our feelings and limitations, we are creating a strong foundation from which to make positive changes in our lives.

In fact we don't need to prove our worth to anyone. Each of us has intrinsic value as a unique human being, although we can lose sight of this during the bad times. We need to stop being so hard on ourselves and constantly remember that, despite our human failings, we are doing the best we know how.

Accepting ourselves as we are does not mean that we become complacent or resigned to our situation. It just means we will stop beating ourselves up for the way our lives are now. Instead of wasting our energy blaming and berating ourselves for being less than perfect, we can use this energy for our own support and care.

Caring for yourself

The idea of self-care is foreign to many women. Socialised to attend to everyone else's needs ahead of our own, there is often little time or energy left to consider our needs, let alone meet them. This is especially true for women in destructive relationships, where the demands are excessive and the rewards few.

Caring for yourself may seem self-indulgent, but if you don't do it, who will? Realising you are worthy of care is an important first step. Next, develop the habit of recognising your needs and satisfying them whenever possible. Ask yourself often, 'What do I need now?', and allow yourself the time and space to do the things that will nurture you. Even if those things are small at first, this is the beginning of affirming your worth.

Exercise: What makes you feel good?

Write a list of at least ten things that uplift and nurture you. Simple and inexpensive possibilities include:

- taking a warm scented bath;
- spending time in the garden;
- sitting in the sun and enjoying nature;
- listening to your favourite music;
- reading an inspirational book;
- phoning a friend;
- getting some exercise;
- doing something creative that gives you pleasure;
- going to the movies;
- having a massage.

Make a commitment to treat yourself to one or more of these things every day. You deserve it!

Take care of your physical needs

When we are stressed, we sometimes undermine ourselves further by unthinkingly neglecting our physical needs.

> I was so skinny and I was smoking sixty cigarettes a day. I can still see myself in the laundry doing the washing with a cigarette hanging out of my mouth. Then I got this rash all over my body: that's how finely tuned I was. My body was really telling me something.

When we neglect our physical needs our emotional distress is often compounded. Regular exercise, sleep and nourishing meals replenishes the energy we so vitally need.

Good nutrition

Some women find it difficult to eat when under stress, while others use food as comfort. Our bodies need and deserve regular nourishment, not binging or starving. If you are having difficulties with compulsive eating, anorexia or bulimia ask your doctor to refer you to an agency or group that can offer you skilled help in overcoming this.

Maintaining a balanced diet can help to keep us emotionally balanced. Try to keep sugar-laden and junk food to a minimum and increase your intake of protein: meat, fish, chicken, lentils, nuts, wholegrains and eggs. Take a multivitamin supplement and vitamin B for stress. Cut down your intake of coffee, tea, chocolate and cola drinks, too. The caffeine in these stimulates the adrenal glands to secrete hormones that signal a body-wide state of emergency. These drinks give us a quick pick-up, but the body is then left even more depleted.

The benefit of exercise

Many women find that getting some form of regular exercise makes them feel more powerful mentally, as well as physically. Exercise helps to counteract depression by stimulating certain hormones in the brain.

> I took out a gym membership and started exercising several times a week. It was my way of coping. That was when I started to get stronger. After I'd exercised I'd seem to be on a high, and that got me through a lot. Frank didn't like it, but I did.

Even if you are unable to participate in strenuous exercise, gentle exercise such as walking or swimming is just as beneficial.

Sleep

If we are short of sleep we will find it difficult to cope. Even if our partner will let us get enough sleep – and many controlling men won't – insomnia can become a problem when we are under stress. Sleep is difficult while the body and mind remain in an aroused and anxious state. If we have young children who require attention at night, we are likely to be perpetually short of sleep anyway. In these situations it is important to schedule daytime naps whenever possible. Make these a priority, not just something you fit in when all other household tasks are completed. To help you unwind before bed-time, take a hot bath, do some stretching exercises, have a hot milky drink or do some light reading. Also limit your caffeine intake.

Reduce your tension

Our breath is our link with life. When we feel fearful and

distressed, our breathing often becomes very shallow and restricted. This is an unconscious attempt to stop ourselves feeling our inner pain. Practising relaxation techniques reduces our stress levels and helps us to feel more centred and connected to our inner strength.

Breathing more fully is a powerful way of diffusing tension, calming our emotions and relaxing our bodies. The following exercise will help you to achieve this.

Exercise: Breathing and centring

Sit or lie quietly and become aware of the rhythm of your breathing. Count the seconds you take to breathe in, to hold your breath and to breathe out. The counting acts as a focus to hold your attention.

Begin to breathe more fully and slowly. Let yourself relax more with each breath. Continue the counting and gradually increase the time you take for each stage of the breath. Aim to build up to the point where you can count to ten on the inward breath, hold that breath for the count of ten and release it to the count of ten. As you become absorbed in your breathing allow yourself to relax mentally and emotionally.

Exercise: Revitalise yourself with a rainbow

This is a simple, quick and yet very powerful exercise to use when you need to soothe yourself.

Relax and take several long, slow, deep breaths. Visualise a beautiful rainbow in front of you. Notice all the colours which are part of that rainbow, and the way they complement one another and blend together.

Now imagine the rainbow slowly beginning to spiral around and around you, until you are completely surrounded by its beautiful healing energy. Bathe in the swirls of colour and breathe deeply and fully. Imagine that each cell in your body is drawing in and absorbing all the colour it needs to renew itself. Continue to bathe in those colours for several minutes. From the rainbow of colours comes new energy and strength.

The importance of feelings

Our feelings are the internal messages that reflect who we really are. When we deny them, we deny ourselves. When we are in pain, that pain is a signal that some aspect of our life needs attention. If we allow ourselves to hear its message, we are in a position to do something about it.

Many of us have trouble identifying what we feel. When in pain, we do our best to numb our feelings by stuffing them deep inside: if we don't feel, we won't hurt. We attempt to anaesthetise ourselves by overworking, watching television, eating, drinking, taking tranquillisers or sleeping. The trouble is, when we numb our distressing feelings, we also numb our positive ones. Gradually we lose our capacity to feel joy, happiness or even hope. And repressed feelings don't go away. Instead they go underground, where they continue to fester. Eventually these bottled-up feelings may be expressed in depression, illness or angry explosions. Unacknowledged feelings may also drive us to act in ways that we later regret.

Denied feelings can seem so intensely overwhelming that we are afraid they will engulf us if we acknowledge them. Surprisingly, the opposite is true. When we acknowledge strong feelings, they begin to subside.

There are three stages to successfully confronting and moving through intense feelings. First, we need to gain an *awareness* of what it is we are feeling. Secondly, we need to *acknowledge* that feeling fully to ourselves and, if possible, to another person. Thirdly, we need to *accept* that feeling as our unique and valid response to our world.

We have been taught that certain feelings such as anger, rage and hate are unacceptable, but experiencing these emotions is part of being human. Denying the feelings we consider unacceptable just makes them push harder for expression. Instead of repressing these feelings, we can accept them yet choose not to act on them in ways that are harmful to other people.

Acknowledge your anger

We have every right to be absolutely furious when someone

is mistreating us. The problem is, it is often not safe to express our anger directly to an abusive partner. Most of us instead go to great lengths to deny, control or redirect our anger.

When you are angry with your partner, what do you usually do with that anger? Do you:

- become angry at yourself instead;
- use an outlet for it, such as house-cleaning or exercise;
- tell someone else how you are feeling;
- take it out on other people, such as your children;
- use food, alcohol or drugs to numb your anger;
- express it directly to your partner?

Does your way of dealing with anger serve you, or does it result in you behaving destructively toward yourself or other people?

Sometimes we are so intent on keeping the peace or so cut off from our feelings that we are not aware of our anger. If you are not aware of feeling angry when your partner hurts you, how do you feel instead?

- Sad?   • Resentful?   • Bitter?   • Guilty?
- Numb?   • Helpless?   • Frightened? • Bewildered?

There may be a number of reasons why we deny or keep the lid on our anger. Which reasons do you relate to?

- I hate my anger, it makes me feel guilty and ashamed.
- I don't want to rock the boat. I just want peace and quiet.
- Getting angry seems like a waste of energy because I never win anyway.
- I'm afraid my anger will push me over the edge into craziness.
- I'm afraid I'll lose control and say or do things I'll regret.
- I'm terrified my partner will leave if I take a stand.
- I know my partner will retaliate if I show my anger.
- I can't cope with his anger so I don't want to risk provoking it.
- I'm frightened he'll get violent if I upset him.
- I'm afraid if I acknowledge my anger I'll have to do something about it.

Although bottling up anger can seem like a solution to these fears, the cost to our well-being is high. Repressed anger drains energy and causes physical tension which can eventually damage our health. It is commonly believed that anger turned against the self causes depression. For the sake of our well-being, our anger needs to be directed where it belongs: at our partner's destructive behaviour.

Anger can be the source of energy and strength we vitally need. When we allow ourselves to feel angry, we are stepping out of defeat and into personal power. For this reason it is important to give ourselves the permission and space to express our anger, however frightening that may feel. This does not mean we need to act on our anger or even communicate it directly to our partner. That may not be safe. Anger can be expressed and released in many ways which do not involve our partner.

Strategies for expressing anger

- *Physical release:* Any kind of physical activity can be beneficial in releasing anger. Try any form of physical exercise, pillow-pounding, hitting a chair with a rolled-up newspaper, kicking and stomping, or taking a dance class or a self-defence course.
- *Emotional release:* Imaginary conversations with your partner when you are in your car or alone at home can help to release your emotions. Tell him how angry you are at his violation of your rights and just what you think of him. You may also find shouting under the shower or in the car with the windows rolled up a good release. Beware of reducing this anger to tears as this moves you back into helplessness.
- *Writing:* Expressing your anger in writing can be a powerful release. Try writing your partner a letter describing his unjust behaviour and telling him exactly how angry it makes you feel. Do this as strongly as you like. This letter is not for his eyes: it is simply an outlet for you to express your grievances. When you have finished, destroy the letter.

If you believe it is safe to do so, you may choose to express your anger directly to your partner. This can be empowering, provided you feel strong enough to stand your ground. When doing this try making a simple statement which begins with 'I' and names your feeling, followed by identifying why you are feeling like that. You may also like to declare the change you would like and the action you will take if there is no change. For example: 'I feel angry when you humiliate me in front of other people and I would like you to stop doing this. If you do this in future I will get up and leave the room.' Chapter 10, 'Reclaiming Your Equality Within the Relationship', contains many other strategies for dealing directly with your partner. In particular see 'Taking a stand', p. 163.

Your wounding self-talk

Being subjected to frequent criticisms and put-downs is akin to brainwashing, so that it is natural that over time we begin to absorb our partner's hurtful words and believe them to be true. Eventually most of us begin to use these same words against ourselves, thus perpetuating our partner's abuse. The way this happens is often insidious.

> I began to listen to the voices in my head and notice how harsh they were. I soon realised that many of those messages were not mine. Some came from the past, from my parents and teachers, and many of them were Mike's. Then I noticed that each night I'd start criticising myself before he got home. I'd walk around the house saying to myself, 'What have you been doing all day? Look at the mess', setting myself up by using his words against myself. Or I'd lie in bed thinking, 'What's the matter with me? I never feel like sex.' Five minutes later he'd say the same thing to me. It was like his criticism had got into my thoughts.

We may not be able to stop our partner's wounding words, but we do have the power to stop our own. Most of the time our inner dialogue goes on unnoticed and unchallenged. We often upset or undermine ourselves without even being aware that we are doing it. Gaining an awareness of our destructive inner messages is the first step in challenging and changing them.

Exercise: Noticing self-wounding words

Think of a recent incident with your partner during which you were self-critical and self-blaming, and reflect on the following questions:
- What critical messages was I giving myself during that incident?
- Who has previously said the same things to me?
- How did this self-talk make me feel?
- How did I act as a result?

Your supportive self

As well as our critical inner voice, we have a supportive inner voice that speaks to us gently and offers us protection and encouragement. This voice may be so faint that we are scarcely aware of it.

> A little voice has been with me for the whole of my life, saying, 'It's all right. It's all right.' That voice keeps me in touch with the positive and gives me hope.

We can usually readily access this supportive self on someone else's behalf. If a friend came to us in distress, we would give her our full compassion and support, but we don't think to offer ourselves that same caring. To strengthen ourselves, we need to make a conscious effort to listen to the inner voice of our supportive self and allow it to give us as much love, care and protection as we would be willing to give a frightened child or our dearest friend.

Exercise: Listening to your supportive self

Refer back to the previous incident, but this time ask yourself:
- What could my supportive self say to me in this situation?
- How does that make me feel?
- How could I act if I listened to this voice?

Improve your self-image

Our self-image defines the limits of who we believe we are and what we perceive we are capable of. Our self-image is not fixed and permanent: it is a changeable creation of our mind. When we change the way we think about ourselves we change our self-image, and that changes the way we act in any given situation.

Deep inside are all the fine qualities that we could ever have – some forgotten, many as yet undiscovered. We can easily forget this when we are overwhelmed by the negative labels that are put on us by our partner and ourself.

To improve your self-esteem, clarify your negative beliefs about yourself and release them. Focus instead on your strengths. The following two exercises will guide you through this process. Do them often and you will notice a dramatic improvement in the way you feel about yourself.

Exercise: Release your negative self-image

Write on the top of a sheet of paper: 'The things I most dislike about myself are . . .' List everything you can think of without censoring. If the thought comes into your mind, write it down. When you have finished, look at your list and ask yourself:

- Where did these beliefs about myself come from?
- Am I using my partner's labels to put myself down?
- Do I want to keep believing these self-criticisms, or am I willing to give them up for the sake of my own well-being?

Now cross off all the statements on your list that your partner has used against you. Then cross out all the statements you use against yourself because of the way your partner's behaviour makes you feel. Finally cross off any other negative statements about yourself that you are willing to let go of. If there are any statements left on your list, check to see if these are compassionate statements of fact, or harsh judgemental criticisms. Rewrite the harsh statements in gentler terms on a separate piece of paper. This can be kept as a reminder of the areas of your life you may like to work on in the future. Alternatively you may choose to work on accepting these things as part of who you are. (See 'The power of self-acceptance', p. 110).

Now imagine the first piece of paper represents an old part of your self-image which you no longer want. Burn this paper and as you watch it burn, concentrate on releasing those negative messages.

Exercise: Name your strengths

We often forget the many positive qualities that may have been temporarily crushed by the abuse we are suffering. Do the following exercise often to remind you who you really are.

Write on the top of a sheet of paper 'I am . . .'

- Now begin to list all the positive qualities you can identify in yourself right now. Don't worry if you are not in touch with many of them. Start an on-going list which you can add to as you remember.

- Next add to your list all the positive qualities you had in the past. Scan your memory for different family, work, relationship and childhood situations where your positive qualities were to the fore. Even if you are not in touch with that quality in yourself now, be assured that if you had it then, it is still there.

- Now project yourself forward in time and think of how you would like to be. Write these qualities down as if they were in the present. Time is irrelevant, because all these qualities you seek are already inside you.

- Finally think of other people – friends and acquaintances and even celebrities and characters from books and films – who have qualities you admire. Identify what it is about them you appreciate, and claim those qualities for yourself by writing them on your list.

Most of our best qualities are often lying dormant when we are in a destructive relationship, but when we name and focus on those qualities they begin to come to the fore again. As you do this exercise, you will probably find that negative thoughts come into your mind. This resistance is just part of the process of change. Acknowledge this reaction gently, and proceed regardless. Before long you will begin to identify with what you write. Make a point of re-writing and reading your list often.

Words that strengthen you

Our words have a powerful effect on us. They shape and reinforce our beliefs about ourselves and the world around us. Because of the effect of past negative experiences, our beliefs are often inaccurate, limiting and destructive. These limiting beliefs can be challenged and changed by consciously stopping our negative thoughts and words, and substituting them for more positive ones.

Affirmations are positive statements which we can repeat in order to change our limiting beliefs. They are a very simple yet powerful way of opening the mind to new possibilities. To be effective they should be short, straightforward and set in the present tense, as if they were already part of our lives. Affirmations can be written, spoken, played on tapes or sung. Repetition of affirmations is the key to success. There are an infinite number of affirmations you can use. The following five are empowering ones to start with.

- I am committed to myself.
- I have the power to protect myself.
- I deserve to be treated with respect and love.
- I give myself the love and care I need.
- I believe in myself.

At first you may feel some resistance to accepting these new ideas. Your 'logical' mind may argue back in disbelief. But as you continue to focus on the positive beliefs, the resistance will diminish surprisingly quickly. Over time the new beliefs will gradually become part of your world, and this opens the door to new possibilities.

Take control of your thoughts

Because the abusive relationship is so bewildering, it is easy to become involved in thinking about it constantly. When the same thoughts are continually going around in our minds but bringing us no closer to a solution, they become destructive.

> Warren would storm out of the house in the morning and I'd be left with everything churning around in my

head. What was the matter? What had I done wrong to upset him? Why was he behaving like this? How could I make it better? How could I make him see I hadn't meant to upset him? I'd go round and round in circles, but really I was getting nowhere and nothing was changing.

Worrying incessantly about the relationship is a time-consuming habit that feeds fear. Breaking that habit can give us time and energy to put into building our relationship with ourselves.

Exercise: Becoming aware of your worry habit

Breaking the worry habit requires determination. Begin to notice thoughts and fears that are repeatedly playing in your head. To make yourself more conscious of them, write them down. Reflect on your worry habit by asking yourself the following questions:

- How much time and energy am I spending on worry over the relationship?
- How realistic are my worries?
- Is my worry serving any useful purpose, or is it just undermining me further?
- What could I do instead of worrying that would help me to feel stronger?

Strategies for dealing with obsessional worry

- Make a conscious decision to work at decreasing the amount of time you spend thinking about the relationship. Count the number of times you think about your partner per hour and work at gradually reducing it.
- Break into your worry by telling yourself 'Stop' every time you notice you have slipped back into it. If you persist with this, you will soon notice a reduction in the number of times you lapse into worry.
- Allot yourself a 'worry time' when you will do nothing but worry about the relationship. It can be surprisingly difficult to worry to a specific timetable and a relief to know you can put it off until a particular time.

- Set aside a specific time to work productively on your concerns. Talk them through with someone else and ask that person to help you plan a strategy to deal with what is worrying you.

The release of writing

Writing can be an excellent way of gaining access to our inner wisdom and clarity, and of making sense of what is happening to us. As we pour our frustrations and fears, thoughts and insights, sadness and hope on to the page, we are expressing our own truth to ourselves. Writing is a safe way of defining our experiences and making them tangible.

> Writing things made them real. It was my way of dealing with them. Like, this is how it really is for me, but I don't actually have to tell anyone about it if I don't want to. I needed to have some way of letting it out, or my head would have exploded. I filled books and books and books.

Many of the exercises in this book recommend writing. For some women the thought of writing can evoke feelings of inadequacy and unpleasant memories of school or other people's criticisms. But the writing exercises in this book are special, because they are just for you. When you write for yourself, the spelling, grammar and punctuation are irrelevant. All that matters is that you express yourself in the way that is right for you. You may choose to use incomplete sentences or lists, or just to note down random, unrelated thoughts. You may decide to use pencil so your words do not seem so permanent. You may prefer to express yourself with poetry or art.

A journal can become like a cherished confidant, there for you whenever you need it. It will be important to find somewhere safe to keep it, perhaps even out of the house. If you do not have access to a safe place, consider disposing of your writing as you go. It can be good to keep your writing to re-read, but this is not absolutely necessary. The main benefit is the clarity and release you gain at the time of writing. Those insights will remain with you.

Exercise: Expressing your thoughts

Getting started is often the most difficult part of writing. Try allowing yourself a ten-minute period in which to write down whatever thoughts run through your mind. Before you begin to write, take a few moments to centre yourself. Close your eyes and take several long, slow, deep breaths. Focus your attention inwards and imagine you are centred in your heart. Spend a few moments getting in touch with your feelings. When you are ready, let your writing flow uncensored and unjudged. Once the flow begins you will probably be surprised at the clarity of what you express. We can learn a lot about ourselves when we take the time to express our thoughts in this way.

Going within

It is possible to create inside you a private space where you can go to reconnect with your self. The following visualisation will guide you in this. If you are not used to using your mind in this way, it may take some practice before you gain a clear sense of this inner retreat. However, once it has been created, your healing retreat is there for you permanently, and it becomes increasingly easy to take yourself there.

Visualisation exercise: Reconnecting with your life force

Begin to breathe deeply and fully. Relax more and more with every breath. Allow yourself to become absorbed in the rhythm of your breathing. Imagine you are breathing in peace and breathing out tension. Know that you are safe. Let go and sink deep within. Imagine you are standing in front of a door. Inside is your own secret room, a safe place that only you have access to. As you open the door and enter, you have a feeling of total security and peace and you hear the words, 'Welcome home.' Your retreat is a place of beauty and comfort. It may contain certain treasured possessions. It may open out onto a beautiful natural scene. Create your retreat just as you want it.

In the centre of the room a bright fire burns on the hearth. This is your own life force: the inner light that is you. Notice how strongly it burns and how full of power it is. Bask in the beautiful light. Breathe in the energy and love which the flames are giving out.

There is a sense of timelessness and permanence about this fire which burns on regardless of external events. In this place, at this time, everything is all right. Spend some time just soaking up the peace. Relax as the warmth spreads through every cell in your body, replenishing your inner emptiness. While you are here you might like to give yourself these affirmations:

- I am strengthened by my inner light.
- I reclaim my personal power.
- I trust my passion and power.

This chapter has suggested ways to rebuild and strengthen your relationship with your self. As we begin to give ourselves some of the care and attention we usually lavish on our partner, our sense of self-worth and personal power begin to expand.

Chapter Eight

The Impact On Our Children

All children are born to grow, to develop, to live, to love, and to articulate their needs and feelings for their self-protection.

— From *For Your Own Good*, Alice Miller

The thought that our children may be suffering is the most painful possibility for most of us to consider. The sad fact is that many of them are. As hard as we try, it is impossible to shield our children completely from the effects of an abusive partner's control. Children tend to soak up everything that is going on around them, whether they are directly involved or not, and may be affected more than we realise. Hearing or seeing their mother being abused, and feeling powerless to help, may be as destructive to the children as being directly abused themselves. The following memories shared by a thirteen-year-old girl help to highlight these facts.

> When he first came to live with us he was really nice and we liked him heaps, but as soon as we went to live in his house he started to lay down the law and turn nasty. He used to get upset over simple little things and just go off the handle. He could be so nice one minute and so awful the next. It was frightening. When he was nasty to me it made me feel like a bit of dirt.
>
> He'd usually fight with Mum when we were in bed. I used to go to my sister's room, and we'd sit there and cry together because we just couldn't understand what was happening. I was scared because I felt that the way he was, he could just whack Mum across the head or anything. He never did hit her, but he would get uptight

like he was going to . . . The thing I found most difficult was when my sister would say, 'Why is he so angry at Mummy?' and I just couldn't tell her because I didn't know. It was my sister I felt most sorry for, because she was only six, and I thought how awful it would be at her age not to know what was going on and to feel like nobody loves you. She was having a real hard time at school because she was upset all the time.

I felt like we were on our own and there was nothing anyone else could do for us. I was only nine and I thought we were going to be there for ever because Mum loved him. I tried to talk to her but she didn't want to talk about it. I think it made her sad. She used to get grumpy easily. She was probably scared for us and scared for herself as well . . . Sometimes I'd think about the things I should've said to him, but I couldn't, because I was so frightened that he'd turn around and hit me.

When we left, that was the worst feeling I had ever had. I was so scared because I thought that he might come home and find us leaving and blow his top. After we left I started having bad dreams about him coming and cutting Mum's head off . . . When we were with him I thought things weren't really that bad. Now when I look back I see that they were worse than I thought. Now I realise that we shouldn't have had to put up with that. It just wasn't fair. I don't like to look back on that time. It's a bad memory I'd rather forget, but I just can't.

How children adapt

Our children are usually just as torn and confused as we are, and they suffer in much the same way. Just as we have changed to cope with our situation, they also adapt. Like us, they may become watchful, anxious to please, afraid to express themselves, tell lies or become depressed. They may also have similar feelings of fear, guilt, anger and shame. Their self-esteem is battered, just as ours is.

Individual children's tolerance to stress differs, and their suffering may be manifested in different ways. Many begin to imitate the behaviour they see around them, especially that of the parent of the same sex. Boys may display aggressive, standover tactics, while girls may become more passive and compliant. Some children will become overly responsible and take on the role of their mother or father's confidant, or other siblings' protector. Some children become withdrawn and quiet. All of these behaviours can be a result of the child's distress.

> *If a child lives with criticism,*
>   *he learns to condemn.*
> *If a child lives with hostility,*
>   *he learns to fight.*
> *If a child lives with ridicule,*
>   *he learns to be shy.*
> *If a child lives with shame,*
>   *he learns to feel guilty.*
> *If a child lives with tolerance,*
>   *he learns to be patient.*
> *If a child lives with encouragement,*
>   *he learns confidence.*
> *If a child lives with praise,*
>   *he learns to appreciate.*
> *If a child lives with fairness,*
>   *he learns justice.*
> *If a child lives with security,*
>   *he learns to have faith.*
> *If a child lives with approval,*
>   *he learns to like himself.*
> *If a child lives with acceptance and friendship,*
>   *he learns to find love in the world.*

– 'Children Learn What They Live',
Dorothy Law Noble.

How are your children coping?

- Do your children often appear tense, worried or frightened?
- Can you see ways in which your children are changing to fit their home situation?

- Are your children beginning to treat you as your partner does?
- Have you noticed your children showing any of the signs of stress listed below?

Symptoms of a child in distress

- isolation, loneliness, withdrawal from others;
- excessive shyness, poor self-esteem, self-loathing;
- fear of the abusive person, frozen watchfulness;
- excessive anxiety, irrational fears;
- hostility, aggressive behaviour, acts of violence;
- sleep disturbances, nightmares;
- soiling or bed wetting, especially in an older child or one who has previously been dry (have this medically checked);
- behaving as if they are much younger than their age or regressing to an earlier stage of development;
- excessive over- or under-eating;
- listlessness, excessive crying (with no obvious reason), depression;
- suicidal feelings, suicide attempts;
- over-responsibility, over-achieving, perfectionism;
- fear of leaving their mother unprotected;
- poor concentration, difficulties at school, deteriorating school work;
- secrecy, dishonesty, stealing, delinquency;
- truancy, running away;
- substance abuse, self-mutilation.

Our difficult task

As mothers we have the difficult, if not impossible, task of protecting our children from the impact of a controlling partner. Most of us go to great lengths to do this. We try to keep our children calm and quiet, and constantly caution them to do nothing that could upset him. At the first sign of trouble we send them off to their rooms out of harm's way. We act as a buffer between our children and our partner, often diverting his anger with the children on to ourselves. We may even take a beating to save our child from one.

As mothers we are also the ones who struggle to cope with the children's reactions to what is happening: behaviour problems, learning difficulties, symptoms of distress and feelings of insecurity. We may also have to cope with increasing disrespect and disobedience from our children as they begin to mirror our partner's behaviour.

> Bob treated me just like one of the kids. I was supposed to jump and run and do things exactly like them. He never took any notice of what I said, and anything I told the kids to do Bob would undermine it by countering me. Eventually he got them all to side with him. Then, no matter what I said, they didn't do it. Gradually they just thought I was nutty and wouldn't take any notice of me at all, and I just felt at a total loss to know what to do.

It is not uncommon for children to blame their mothers for the ways they are suffering. They are usually angry, and it is safer to direct their anger at us rather than at the abusive male. They resent the control tactics we use to keep them out of the line of fire. And they often end up blaming us for not leaving and creating a happier and safer life for them. Probably the most heartbreaking thing for any of us to cope with is when our children turn against us and begin to mistreat us.

Under constant pressure, it is no wonder that some of us find it difficult to cope with our children. We may become inattentive and impatient, hostile, explosive or abusive.

It is easy to deflect our pain and anger on to our children. If you are afraid you may harm your child, it is important to seek help. (See pp. 244–58 for community resources that can help.) Writing or reflecting on the following questions may help you decide what to do.

How are you coping with the children?

- Are you so preoccupied with your situation that you are neglecting your children's physical and emotional needs?
- Are you using your children to confide in inappropriately?
- Are you taking your frustrations out on them?

- Are you responding to your child as you do your partner?
- Have there been times when you have been afraid of harming your children?
- Do you need to seek help?

If you are not coping with the children

- *Take time out.* Tell your children that you are not available, and leave the room. Spend time doing something to relieve your stress: exercise, deep breathing, crying, screaming or hitting the bed.
- *Get support for yourself.* Ring someone who cares about you and talk through what is happening and how that is making you feel. Ask her or him for the support you need.
- *Involve other people.* Arrange for relatives and friends to spend time with the children. This can help to take the pressure off you, and get some of the children's needs met as well.
- *Seek help.* There are crisis phone lines and many social service agencies that are run by caring people who will offer you support. (For details, see pp. 244–58.) Many communities run parenting courses which can provide invaluable support, information and new friendships.

Sometimes, even when we are coping with our children's distress, we are at a loss to know how to help them to deal with their situation. These suggestions may help.

Strategies for reducing children's distress

- *Reassure the children* frequently that the problems in the home are not their fault. Children usually believe they are in some way to blame.
- *Listen carefully* to your children's fears and concerns. This lets them know they are important, validates their experience and helps them to come to terms with how they are feeling.
- *Encourage them to talk through their feelings.* Children have a right to all their feelings, including anger. Feelings that are bottled up often come out later in destructive ways. If you feel shocked by or disagree with their perceptions,

try saying, 'I didn't know you felt like that.' This validates their feelings in a neutral way.

- *Hug your children, and tell them often that you love them.* Children need a lot of reassurance when their world feels insecure. Don't be afraid to apologise to them if you have been unfair to them.
- *When you feel unable to give your children the attention and affection they need, reassure them that this is temporary and not their fault.* Explain that right now you are feeling upset and need some time for yourself.
- *Be honest with your children about what is happening* in the home. Children take in a lot more than we think. Your denial or secrecy can make them doubt their perceptions and leave them feeling confused.
- *Restrict your discussion to a simple explanation.* Children may be reassured if you simply tell them that it is not right for people to hurt one another, and that you are trying to sort the situation out.
- *Don't overburden children* by treating them as confidants or expecting them to solve your problems. When children are involved in adult issues which they are powerless to change, it makes them anxious.
- *Build your children's self-esteem* and confidence by praising their efforts, however small. Praise helps children to believe in themselves.
- *Direct any criticism at the children's behaviour, not their self-image.* Rather than saying, 'You're stupid', say, 'I don't like it when . . .'
- *Encourage your children to spend time with loving and reliable relatives or friends.* This will give them access to other types of family relationships in which they can receive quality attention in a stress-free environment.
- *Support them in getting involved in activities outside the home* that will build their self-esteem.
- *Ensure that the children know exactly what to do and where to go for help* if your partner is likely to become violent. Make sure they have the phone numbers of the police, relatives and neighbours they may need to contact. Tell them to put their safety first, and

let them know that it is not their job to try to protect you.

- *Be alert to signs of distress and be prepared to leave in order to protect your children* if it becomes necessary. They are dependent on you for their well-being.

Involving other people

- Back-up and support is important. Where possible, involve the members of both your own and your partner's family in what is happening. Consider having an arrangement whereby they will collect the children if there is a blow-up.
- If possible, arrange with neighbours for the children to go to them if you need to get them out of the house. Don't be afraid to ask. People are often glad to help when they realise your predicament.
- If the child is distressed, it is important to let the school know that there is stress at home and that it is affecting the child. Teachers appreciate knowing this, and may make allowances for any disruptive behaviour. It can also be helpful to speak to other sports and hobby group leaders who are involved with your child. There is no need to give more details than you feel comfortable with.

When your partner becomes abusive toward your children

Child physical abuse is a pattern of physical mistreatment and non-accidental injury which includes: hitting with an object, shaking, slapping, punching, hair-pulling, pinching, kicking, throwing, arm-twisting, burning or beating. Most of us are aware when our partner has overstepped the mark and is physically abusing our children. We are not nearly so clear about where the boundaries are with emotional abuse. Any behaviour that repeatedly undermines the child's self-confidence is emotionally abusive. This includes: ignoring, mocking, name-calling, criticising, badgering, shouting, intimidating and terrorising.

Many people believe that emotional abuse is less damaging than physical abuse. The fact is, it can be even more harmful. A child's self-image is developed by the messages she or he receives from other people. Constant negative messages are destructive. Over time, hurtful labels like 'dumb', 'stupid', 'crazy', 'useless' and 'hopeless' are believed, and can crush the child's fragile self-esteem. The wounds can last a lifetime.

Many men who abuse their partners also abuse their children. This places the woman in a terrible dilemma. How can she protect her children when sometimes she cannot even protect herself? Often the answer is: she can't.

> When our daughter was ten Greg used to get hold of her and say, 'Your mother's crazy.' At first she'd say, 'No, Mum's not crazy', but he'd shake her and shake her and keep on saying it until finally she'd say, 'Yes, Mum is crazy.' Then he'd let her go and say to me, 'See, I told you so, you're crazy.' I'd try to stop him doing it, but he'd just push me out of the way and shout me down, saying it wasn't any of my business.

You may have reached the stage where you feel too frightened and powerless to intervene when your partner is abusing the children. That is the time when some women enlist the help of family members, friends or church elders to try to convince their partner to seek help. If this doesn't work, you need seriously to consider leaving. Your children are vulnerable and they are totally dependent on you to protect them.

Do your children need protection?

- Is your partner abusing the children in any of the ways listed above?
- What outside help can you get that you haven't already tried?
- Realistically, are you able to protect your children while living under the same roof as your partner, or do you need to consider leaving?

Child sexual abuse

In recent years the secrecy that has surrounded child sexual abuse has finally been broken. As more and more people share their experiences of childhood sexual abuse, we are realising just how common it is. As a protection against abuse, all children need to be taught, from a young age, the difference between safe and unsafe touching. They need to know that their body is their own and they have the right to say no to other people's touch. There are some community courses available on how to teach your child to stay safe from sexual abuse.

Some men who abuse their families in other ways also sexually abuse one or more of the female or male children in that family. The term sexual abuse refers to any kind of adult involvement with a child for the purpose of the adult's sexual gratification. This may include non-physical actions such as invading the child's privacy by watching her wash or dress, making sexually suggestive remarks, having the child pose for sexually explicit photos, or exposing the child to pornography. Physical actions of abuse include: inappropriate kissing or tickling; oral sex; touching the child's genitals or having the child touch his; penetration of the child's genitals with objects, fingers or a penis.

The adult is always 100 per cent responsible for child sexual abuse. Whether the child is coerced or bribed into the abusive situation, and whether she or he appears to have consented, it is never the child's fault. The adult is the one with the responsibility and power. There is *never* any excuse for the abuse of that power.

If a child is being sexually abused, she or he may display any of the symptoms of distress listed on p. 130. She or he may also show some of the following signs:

Possible symptoms of sexual abuse

- Pain, injury or infection in the genital, anal or oral areas;
- excessive masturbation or interest in other people's genitals (with the emphasis on the word excessive);
- knowledge about sexual acts which is too sophisticated for the child's developmental age;

- acting out sexually abusive behaviour with toys, animals or other children;
- frequent headaches, stomach aches, psychosomatic or stress-related illnesses.

If you have any reason to suspect that your child is being sexually abused, it is essential that you act to protect them immediately. Sexual abuse can have a destructive impact on the child for a lifetime. As soon as you can, talk to the child about safe and unsafe touching, and give the child the opportunity to tell you if any unsafe touching has occurred.

When a child does disclose sexual abuse, the usual reaction for a parent is shock and disbelief. If the parent has herself been abused as a child, and has not acknowledged or healed from that, the disclosure is particularly traumatic. In this situation it is natural to want to deny our child's abuse, just as we deny the impact of our own. It is important not to do this. (See 'Healing past wounds', p. 213.) The following guidelines are recognised as helpful in dealing with the initial impact of the child's disclosure.

If your child tells you she has been sexually abused . . .

- *Believe the child*. Children almost never make up this kind of thing.
- *Stay calm.* Your reaction is very important. The child has taken a risk in telling. If you over-react, the child may be traumatised further. Assure the child that she or he has done the right thing in telling you.
- *Reassure the child that she or he is not to blame*. Children usually believe they have in some way caused the abuse.
- *Get professional help*. Sexual abuse is a very complex problem that requires careful handling. Contact your local social services or an agency that deals with sexual abuse (see pp. 244–58). They will have specially trained people who will interview the child in a supportive way. They will also help you to plan for the safety of your children and ensure they are not reabused. A medical examination will be arranged for the child if this is thought appropriate.

Although this may show evidence of abuse, in most cases it does not. Lack of medical evidence does not prove the abuse did not take place.

It is devastating to realise that your child has been sexually abused, especially if the abuser is your partner. Healing from such a trauma takes a long time. In the months ahead, you may find some of the following suggestions useful:

- Talk through your feelings with trusted and supportive friends.
- Join a support group for mothers of sexual abuse survivors. (The agency you have been dealing with will be able to give details of any groups in your area.)
- Seek specialised counselling for yourself. It is also advisable to seek counselling for the child.
- Read about how other people have coped. (See pp. 259–63 for suggested books.)

Above all else we want our children to be happy and thriving. It is terribly hard to face the fact that they may not be. We can do our best to make our children's lives as secure as possible, but we need to remember that there is only so much we can do to compensate for our partner's destructive behaviour. Sometimes the only way we can give our children the security they need is by leaving. Parenting alone is a challenge, but at least it allows us to create a safe life for our children.

It's taken a long time to heal my relationship with my kids. They were so angry. They blamed me because their stepfather had been so hard on them. About a year ago we were finally able to bring things out in the open. It was really painful for me to hear how hurt and frightened they'd been, but they did need to be heard. We talked about how bad those times were for all of us, and I told them how sorry I was for all the times when I was too scared to stand up for them. It was quite emotional, and afterwards we all felt much closer. Now things are really good between us. I'm so lucky to have my kids. I used to think that I had to put my relationship with Keith first because the kids were going to grow up and leave, and he'd be all I had. I was so wrong. Keith is long gone, but my children and grandchildren are an important part of my life, really the best part. And they'll always be there.

Chapter Nine

Choosing the Right Path

The agonising question of whether to leave or stay with our partner is faced by most of us eventually. If you are considering this question, you already know there is no simple answer.

The prospect of giving up a relationship, even one fraught with difficulty, is traumatic. Because of the dynamics of abuse we have probably given more, and tried harder, than many other people in good relationships. The more of ourselves we have invested, the more there is at stake, and the harder it is to admit failure. In any case, most of us do not want to give up the life we know, to embark alone on a journey with undeniable hazards and an uncertain destination. If we are at a particularly low ebb, we may feel ill equipped for such a journey.

Even if we know we have to go, it is tempting to postpone the inevitable in the hope that either the relationship will improve or that we will feel more confident about beginning the journey later. The difficulty with this strategy is that our partner's behaviour is probably becoming more controlling while our emotional and physical resources are becoming increasingly depleted. Postponement can leave us feeling even more desperate, with even less energy to cope with the breaking-up and rebuilding process.

With so much at stake it becomes increasingly difficult to reach any decision. We swing back and forth between fleeting hope and utter despair. We often have several voices in our head, giving conflicting messages. This babble adds to our confusion.

I'd decide I definitely had to go, and then I just wouldn't

do anything. I was so incredibly stuck. I'd tell myself, 'I should leave. I've got to leave.' Then I'd panic and say, 'I can't leave.' I went round and round. I knew the reality but I hoped there might be some change. It was frightening, because all the time I was getting weaker, and in the end I became so dispirited I just wanted to crawl under a rock and die.

Eventually we may feel too worn down to make a decision. With no energy to change our situation, we hang on passively long after hope has gone. Or we wait in the hope that the decision will be taken out of our hands by an accident or our partner's voluntary departure. But this rarely happens.

Without intervention the destructive relationship is usually on a downward spiral. You may already have tried a variety of strategies. The harsh reality may be that the only real choice you have is between staying and suffering your partner's abuse, or leaving and facing the frightening prospect of life alone. Undoubtedly the most painful decision of all is to leave when you still love your partner. It is heartbreaking to accept that no amount of loving is ever going to make things right. A one-sided struggle on your part is destined to leave you feeling empty and disillusioned.

The following questions and exercises will provide a framework to help you stand back and evaluate the state of your relationship. Some honest soul-searching will give you a new clarity. As you proceed, try to put on hold your fears about the future. You have the right to choose the path that is right for you.

It may be hard to believe at the moment, but it is possible to move on and find happiness outside the relationship, if that is the choice you make. Keep this in mind as you work your way through this chapter.

Is your partner willing to change?

Unfortunately the majority of controlling men are not prepared to acknowledge the destructive impact of their behaviour, much less work at changing it. If an abusive man promises to change, the only true test of his sincerity is action.

In evaluating your partner's willingness to change, ask yourself:

- Does he accept responsibility for his destructive behaviour?
- What is he prepared to do about it?
- When will he do it?

If your partner is already involved in counselling or a programme, you can assess your partner's progress objectively by completing the checklist 'Measuring your partner's change' (p. 172) on a regular basis.

If your partner is obviously resisting taking responsibility for his actions, a sobering question to ask yourself is:

- Why would he change?

As we have seen, there is often little incentive for our partner to do so. Most abusive men already have what they want: control. They also have the bonus of a partner who is continually trying to please them. Most do not want to give this up, and will resist any action that threatens it.

Soul-searching questions to consider

Reflect deeply on your answers to the following questions. Afterwards you may like to take the three questions that create the strongest reaction in you and write about them in your journal.

- Am I losing more and more of my peace of mind, self-esteem, confidence, self-respect, freedom and/or rights?
- Are the bad times becoming more frequent and more destructive?
- What have I done to improve the relationship?
- What has my partner done to improve the relationship?
- Did these attempts have a positive, lasting effect?
- Am I losing ground emotionally? How do I feel now, compared to six months ago? Twelve months ago? Two years ago?
- Is my physical health suffering because of the stress?
- Do I have any hope that the abusive cycle can be reversed and that I can reclaim my power in the relationship?

- Is staying on, as things are, a viable option?
- If I stay in the relationship, how do I imagine my life will be one year from now? How about five years from now?
- If things continue to get worse, at what point will I go?
- In my heart of hearts, do I really believe that the relationship can be turned around, or does the future with my partner look bleak?

What price are you paying?

Many sacrifices are made and losses incurred by women in destructive relationships. Naming these for yourself can be revealing.

Take a sheet of paper and head it up: 'The Price I Pay For Being in This Relationship Is . . .'

List the costs in all aspects of your life, including your self-esteem, personal development, relationships with other people, health, career, finances, interests, security, freedom, sexuality, future plans and dreams.

When you have finished, ask yourself: 'Is it worth it?'

How close to burnout are you?

As part of your overall decision-making process, it is important to evaluate the effect your partner's behaviour is having on you. None of us can continue to function well under constant pressure. We may cope for a time, but stress is cumulative; the effects build up until eventually symptoms appear. Often we are so intent on coping we fail to recognise these symptoms as warning signs. (See 'Dealing with depression', p. 102.) Breakdown may be the end result of prolonged and unbearable stress.

The following list includes mild and acute symptoms of burnout. Which ones are you currently experiencing, and how often?

Never: 1   *Frequently*: 2   *Occasionally*: 3   *Constantly*: 4

Lack of energy	____	Feelings of anxiety	____
Irritability	____	Chronic worrying	____

Difficulty making decisions	____	Memory lapses	____
Withdrawal from other people	____	Loss of confidence	____
Decreasing enjoyment of life	____	Lack of motivation	____
Working harder but achieving less	____	Crying spells	____
Feeling depressed	____	Changed sleeping patterns	____
Loss of sex drive	____	Changes in food consumption	____
Increased alcohol consumption	____	Misuse of drugs	____
Tension headaches	____	Heart palpitations	____
Allergy flare-ups	____	Other physical symptoms	____
Panic attacks	____	Feeling hopeless about life	____
Sense of helplessness	____	Feeling disconnected from yourself	____
Inability to cope with life	____	Doubts about your sanity	____
Dread of the future	____	Thoughts of suicide	____

The higher the number you score, the closer you are to burnout and the more you need to care for yourself. Refer back to Chapter 6, 'Reaching Out for the Support You Need', and Chapter 7, 'Reconnecting With Your Self', to remind yourself of ways to strengthen and nurture yourself.

To establish whether and how rapidly your mental, emotional and physical health is deteriorating, think back to a time about six months ago. Were you experiencing the same symptoms then? If so, were they more or less severe? Complete the checklist for that time and compare it to how you are feeling now. You can use this checklist as an on-going record in this way if you do decide to stay with your partner.

Is your safety at risk?

You have a right to a life free from intimidation or violence.

If there is a serious risk of harm to you or those you love, it is important to acknowledge it and to take steps to protect yourself and your family. Reflect on the following questions:

- Is my partner becoming increasingly threatening toward me?
- Am I afraid for my own safety or that of others I care about?
- Is my fear stopping me from leaving?

There is a natural tendency to downplay threats and to believe that our partner would never actually harm us. It is dangerous to hold on to this belief when his words tell us otherwise. Today's threats are often tomorrow's reality. (See 'Strategies to ensure your safety . . .', p. 187.)

If you are staying with your partner out of fear, you need to enlist other people's help in planning your escape and in finding a safe place to go. (See 'The role of the Women's Refuge', p. 183, and 'Community Resources', p. 244–58.) Chapter 11, 'The Challenge of Breaking Free', addresses many of the issues that are faced when we leave a relationship.

Are your children suffering?

Despite our efforts to protect them, children are hurt by living with abuse. You will already have reflected on your children's situation while reading the previous chapter. ('The Impact On Our Children,' pp. 127–39.) Now consider the following questions:

- Are there likely to be harmful long-term effects on the children if they continue to live in their current situation?
- Is staying with your partner putting them at risk?
- Do they need your protection?

In order to ease our own pain, our first reaction may be to deny what is happening to our children. This reaction is understandable, but it prevents the real issues being addressed and keeps us stuck in a cycle of denial, guilt and self-blame unable to take action. If your children are suffering any kind of severe abuse, it is essential that you take steps to keep them safe. Many women say that it was when they became aware of how damaging their situation was to their children that they finally found the strength to leave.

Weighing up your options

The following practical exercise can help you to weigh up your options. Think deeply and honestly about how it would be if you did stay with your partner. Take a piece of paper, head it up as follows and write a list of the good points about staying and then the bad. Both sides of your lists need not necessarily be equal – indeed they probably won't be! As we saw in Chapter 5, 'What Stops Us From Leaving?', women's reasons for staying are as diverse as the women themselves. The following lists may be similar or very different to yours.

IF I STAY . . .

The Good Points	*The Bad Points*
Things may improve	Things may get worse
We will still be a couple	I can't stop him mistreating me
I won't have to face life alone	I may have a breakdown
I will have financial security	The kids will suffer
	My partner may become violent

Now think deeply about how it would be if you left. Take a second piece of paper and repeat the process for that situation.

IF I GO . . .

The Good Points	*The Bad Points*
I probably won't have a breakdown	The kids will miss him
I may have a better life	I will have nowhere to go
I will stop hurting	He might hurt me
I will be free	I have a lot to lose financially
The kids will be safe	I will have to start again

Laying out the issues in this way will give you an overall picture of just what is at stake. The risks of staying in your relationship should also be apparent.

Go through your lists and consider how important each point is to you now. Is there any one point that stands out as more important than the others? Is this a key aspect you should be acting on? If possible, talk through the issues raised by these lists with a trusted and understanding friend or a counsellor. If this is not possible, you may like to express your feelings and concerns in your journal.

Trust your feelings

As much as we try to deny them, our feelings are a true response to our situation – and they have probably been painfully churned up by the previous questions. It hurts to probe beneath the surface to face how you truly feel, but by doing this you gain valuable insights into what is really right for you. Notice your internal responses as you consider the following questions.

- When did you last feel deeply loved, cherished and at peace?
- What are your feelings trying to tell you about your situation?

Feeling the pain that these questions may evoke can lead you to a new clarity and sense of connection to yourself which will help you in your decision-making.

Inner wisdom

> *Practise listening to your intuition, your inner voice: ask questions: be curious: see what you see: hear what you hear: and then act on what you know to be true.*
>
> – from *Women Who Run With the Wolves*,
> Clarissa Pinkola Estes

Beyond our logic and our fears there is a wise part of us that knows the right thing to do. This inner guidance, or intuition, connects us to a higher knowledge and wisdom which is usually beyond our conscious awareness. Examples of the way our intuition guides us in our lives include the sudden flash of an idea, a quiet inner whisper, or a gut feeling about the right direction to take. Guidance may also come through dreams, books, things other people say, or even songs.

> I was lying there crying and this song came on the radio. It wasn't like any song I'd ever heard before. The words just went right into me, like it was talking specially to me. I knew it was telling me what I had to do. I now realise it was my inner wisdom. I didn't need to feel chained down any more. It had been four wasted years. Right then I just knew I was the only one who would make that change. Suddenly I felt really strong. All this strength and I didn't even know where it came from. It was just there when I needed it and I could act.

We all have this inner wisdom, but many of us fail to notice its signal, or act without being aware we are following that guidance. We may also block out our inner wisdom because it tells us something we do not want to know. Although it can be frightening to trust it, this guidance works for good in our lives. It is there to protect us.

The first step in being able consciously to use this guidance is to acknowledge that it is there. Remember a time when you experienced a sense of clarity or conviction about what to do.

- What form did this take?
- At that time were you aware that this was a message from your intuition?
- Did you act on it?
- What was the outcome?
- Are you conscious of that guidance in your life now?

In the midst of distress we often become confused by our chaotic thoughts and feelings. It is difficult to distinguish between the message of our intuition and the many internal voices of fear, but they are very different. The guidance of our inner wisdom will always be accepting, encouraging and loving. It will not criticise or condemn us. Even in our confusion, our inner guidance will always be there. Begin to become aware of how your intuition communicates with you in your everyday life.

Acknowledging and learning to trust this guidance is an on-going task that is well worth the effort. There are many wonderful books available on this subject which can help you. As you begin to recognise and act on your intuition, you will be guided on the path that is right for you. Practising the following visualisation will strengthen your connection. It may take many attempts before you feel directly in touch with that wise part of yourself. Don't try to force anything to happen. Just maintain an expectation that you will soon receive the guidance you need. The connection will come if you persist. Tell yourself often, 'My inner wisdom is guiding me toward perfect solutions', and open yourself up to receiving different perspectives and new possibilities.

Visualisation Exercise: Seeking inner guidance

Close your eyes and take several long, slow, deep breaths. Focus your attention inward and each time you breathe out, allow yourself to sink deeper inside. Imagine a multi-coloured waterfall and see yourself beneath it being showered with the colours. Allow yourself to absorb these colours and let them cleanse and soothe you.

Now imagine that you are sitting beside the waterfall. You feel peaceful and safe. Invite your inner guide to join you. Become aware of a loving presence that surrounds you. Recognise it as your guide. You may see your guide as an actual person or just experience it as a comforting presence. Spend a few minutes absorbing this loving energy.

When you are ready, you can speak directly to your guide and ask it to clarify which path is right for you. You may get an immediate response in the form of a feeling, thought, picture or inner voice. If you don't, allow yourself to believe that the right answer will come later. When it does, don't be afraid to follow it.

Chapter Ten

Reclaiming Your Equality Within the Relationship

When the soulful life is being threatened, it is not only acceptable to draw the line and mean it, it is required. When a woman does this, her life cannot be interfered with for long . . .

— from *Women Who Run with the Wolves*,
Clarissa Pinkola Estes

If you have consciously made the choice to stay in your relationship, you are in a far stronger position than before. Regardless of the reasons for your decision, by making a choice you have regained some control over your life. You have committed yourself to staying, but at any time you can re-evaluate your situation and choose again. This knowledge is itself empowering.

Most of us who decide to stay hope we will find a way to stop our partner abusing us. The sad fact is, *we* cannot stop his abuse. *Our partner makes the choice to behave as he does, and only he can decide to change*. Meantime, although we are powerless to change our partner, we do have the power to make personal changes.

There are several changes we could decide to make that will help us to reclaim our equality within the relationship. We can choose to believe in ourselves again, no matter what our partner says. We can begin to distance ourselves emotionally, so that our partner's behaviour no longer has the same power to hurt us. Instead of accepting our partner's restrictions, we may begin to enrich our lives by pursuing our interests outside the relationship. We may try relating to our partner more assertively. We may even decide to take a definite stand and declare we are no longer willing to tolerate our partner's abuse.

This chapter will guide you in exploring a variety of ways to reclaim your equality within your relationship. Each of us will find her own solutions, and we may need to experiment before we find the most appropriate and empowering ones. Before embarking on a course of change it is important to rebuild your self-esteem and sense of personal power. The self-care options suggested in Chapters 6 and 7 will help you to achieve this.

The challenge of change

Deciding to work at reclaiming our equality within an abusive relationship is an act of courage. Change takes us into unknown territory, where we need to face and move with our fears. Our determination and resilience will probably be tested to the limit as we endeavour to make changes in the face of our partner's objections.

> Initiating new behaviours was scary, not because of what I feared from my partner but because it was new, and change is very frightening. I'd worry, 'What is going to happen if I do this?' The old way, I used to know what the outcome of different behaviours and comments would be. It was hard not knowing, letting go of the control and just doing it.

Change within an intimate relationship involves tremendous risk. The stakes are high and there is no way of knowing what the outcome will be. Our partner may learn to treat us with respect and ease up on his control, or if he is determined to continue his control tactics he may ultimately find someone else who will accept his abuse. Our partner's departure can be a distressing possibility to consider.

It is difficult to initiate and maintain change of this magnitude without support. If possible, join a women's support group. An assertiveness group can also help you gain new ideas and skills. (See 'Joining a support group', p. 100.)

Change begins from within. The clearer we can become about our intention to reclaim our power, the greater our chances of doing so. We are in our strongest position when we are willing to risk all we have in order to make changes in our lives.

> I think things began to change for the better when I reached the point of saying, 'I can live without this man if I have to.' There was no way I was going to let him destroy me. The bottom line was, if he didn't shape up, I was out of there. I knew that was the only chance I had for my own survival. Before that I'd been too frightened to take a stand because I thought he'd leave me, but suddenly I just couldn't stand being walked over any more and I was willing to risk it all to stop him. And it was strange, because it was almost like he realised that this time I meant business and he began to back off and take notice of me for a change.

Even if we are not in a position to risk all, we can still take small steps towards change in the knowledge that we can give up our efforts later if we choose to.

Prepare for your partner's resistance

Our partner has a vested interest in keeping things the way they are. If we stand against his control, it is highly likely he will attempt to sabotage our show of strength by increasing his control tactics. It is important to anticipate this.

> Every time I refused to do what Kim wanted, he'd try every trick in the book to bring me into line. It got so I pretty well knew what he'd do next. First he'd try to override me by mocking me; then he'd twist things around and accuse me of being selfish; then he'd become sarcastic and nasty, and finally, when he saw it was hopeless and I wasn't going to back down, he'd go into a sulk. Because I'd started to see his behaviour more clearly, I wasn't dragged into defending myself like I'd been before, and I found it easier to hold out against him. It became almost amusing to stand back and watch

his antics. In a way it even strengthened my resolve to do what I intended.

For some men this reaction is temporary and it will eventually decrease when they realise we intend to stand our ground. For others who are determined to abuse, this resistance will probably increase until we are forced to re-evaluate our position and decide either to back down or leave. We need to be prepared to weather the storm for a time, until we can see which it will be.

If your partner has been physically abusive in the past, or if you are afraid he will resort to violence, the possibility of being able to take a direct stand against him will be limited. Never put your safety at risk. Take only the steps that you judge to be safe. (See 'Strategies for ensuring your safety . . .', p. 187.)

Exercise: Acknowledge and overcome your fear of change

Bringing your fears out in the open helps to make them more manageable. Reflect on, or write about, the following questions:

- What are my greatest fears about attempting to change within the relationship?
- Are these fears realistic?
- Am I willing to take the risk of change despite my fears and my partner's probable resistance?
- How will I support myself through my fears and withstand my partner's attempts to push me back into a powerless position?
- What support will I put in place before I begin?
- If I embark on a course of change, how long will I give it?
- How will I know when it is time to give up?

You may find it helpful to discuss the issues raised by these questions with a friend, support group or counsellor. Other people's objective input is often invaluable. (See also 'Acknowledging and redefining your fears', p. 177.)

Personal change

In placing the focus on your own change, rather than hoping to somehow change your partner, it is helpful to define an ideal of how you would like to be in the relationship. Before attempting to change your external behaviour, it is empowering to reconnect with that part of your inner self that is strong, forthright and able to protect and sustain you.

Visualisation exercise: Creating a powerful self-image

To build a more powerful image of yourself within the relationship, start by asking yourself the following questions:

- If I were to reclaim my equality in this relationship, how would I be different?
- How would I respond to my partner's control?
- What actions would I take?
- What would I say to him and how would I say it?
- What would I be telling myself?
- How would this feel?

Spend time each day visualising your powerful self in action. This is like a mental dress rehearsal. Create imaginary scenarios of interactions with your partner during which you successfully stand your ground. Keep your attention focused on this powerful image of yourself, not on your partner's possible reactions. The more you practise this new behaviour in your mind, the more feasible it becomes, and the more likely you are to bring it into being.

Exercise: Setting your goals

It is important to have an overall vision of the ways in which you would like to reclaim your power. Setting personal goals gives you something positive to aim for.

Write a list of the specific ways you would like to change your behaviour within the relationship. Begin the list: 'Ideally in this relationship I would like to . . .'

Once again be sure to keep the focus on yourself, not on your partner's behaviour. At this stage don't worry about how you are going to make these changes; just open up your mind to the possibility of change. A possible list of goals could include, for example:

- Stop apologising to my partner unnecessarily.
- Attend a women's support group once a week, despite my partner's opposition.
- Stop striving to keep the home to my partner's standards, and keep it to my own instead.
- Get up and leave the room when my partner shouts at me.
- Learn to say 'No' to my partner's demands when I want to, and to stand my ground.
- Stop seeking my partner's approval and give myself approval instead.

It is a good idea to tackle these changes one at a time, and it is often best to start with an easy goal first. Attempts to make and sustain radical changes before we are strong enough can mean they are doomed to failure. (See 'Taking a stand', p. 163.)

Establishing your partner's position

Having decided to stand against your partner's control, your next decision is whether you will discuss this openly with him. This decision is an individual one, which will depend on how strong you are feeling and how abusive your partner is. In my own case, I opted to take a stand without discussion. I already knew my partner was non-negotiable and unavailable for direct communication.

If you decide to initiate a discussion with your partner, the form it takes will depend on your situation. For some women it means sharing their feelings of distress and asking for consideration. For others it is a definite ultimatum: either her partner gets help to overcome his pattern of control, or she leaves. Deciding to speak out directly to your partner can give you a measure of his willingness both to change and to meet you half way with respect and compassion.

The key to my regaining my power has been in my believing I had power. There was a time when I was so burnt out and ill I knew I had to take a stand. I told my partner I could not carry on this way any longer or I would probably end up doing something I'd regret, or even killing myself. There had to be some bottom lines in the relationship. The basic one was, I no longer wanted him to constantly put pressure on me. I wanted to stop acting out of fear and guilt. So many of my reactions weren't even honest, because I was too afraid to be true to myself because of his pressure. I was to be treated with respect; my needs were to be considered; and I no longer wanted to go on in a bland, numb, blind state where I was just going along with everything and surviving. I wanted to be loved and appreciated. Just saying these things was empowering. Taking a stand was a major .shift within myself, because I gave myself courage by doing it. It was so much easier than I thought it would be. And I found to my astonishment that I was met with respect.

The following questions will help you decide whether to initiate an open discussion with your partner:

- Have I confronted my partner about his controlling behaviour before, or have I been suffering in silence?
- Has my partner been open to negotiation in the past?
- Will declaring my intention to change be a helpful first step? Is my partner likely to meet me with respect or attempt to sabotage me?
- Do I feel strong enough to cope with my partner's reactions?
- Will confronting my partner put my safety at risk?

Before initiating a discussion with your partner it is best to clarify in your own mind what you want to say and what you are hoping to achieve. For ideas on how to prepare yourself see 'Strategies for confronting', p. 210.

Regardless of whether your partner agrees to seek help, you can still begin to reclaim your equality in the relationship. As you do, changes will undoubtedly be created.

If your partner is willing to get help

When challenged strongly by their partner, some men agree

to seek help. Unfortunately there is no quick and easy way for a man to change his established pattern of control. It requires not only a willingness to face up to his behaviour, but also an on-going commitment to work at changing it. If your partner is willing to take responsibility and make that commitment, then there is certainly reason to hope. If he is not, the prognosis is poor.

Under threat of their partner leaving, some men begin to go through the motions of seeking help without any real intention of changing. Some even take what they learn and twist it around to endorse their own position.

> I recall my partner enrolling in an anger management course and I thought, 'This will be the answer.' On the second night he came home with a grin from ear to ear and said, 'The instructor says I'm normal because everyone gets angry, it's only natural.' It was like a knife had been stuck right through my heart. I knew it was hopeless and I was fighting a losing battle.

The starting place for any real personal growth is honesty and self-responsibility. Without this, our controlling partner will not be able to make real changes in his attitude and behaviour.

Attending a non-violence group is probably the best option for a man who is willing to work at change. These groups cater for men who are verbally, emotionally, sexually or physically abusive toward their partner as these are all considered to be forms of violence. The aim is to have the man recognise that his control is exercised in many ways, including: putdowns, intimidation, threats, isolation, treating their partner like a servant, financial deprivation, manipulation of children, and violence. These programmes work toward having the man acknowledge this fact and examine the attitudes that underlie his abuse. When a man takes responsibility for changing his beliefs about male superiority and his right to control his partner, lasting change can take place. Without this, superficial changes to behaviour are often short-lived.

If a man has a problem with substance abuse he may agree to attend a special programme to help him change. Overcoming substance abuse can make a difference, but we need to be aware that the issue of our partner's abuse toward us and the attitudes that underlie this will usually not be addressed in the programme. This means that even if our partner overcomes his addiction, his controlling behaviour will probably still continue. (See 'It's because of the alcohol/drugs', p. 68.)

Some men will not attend a group, but will agree to go to counselling. As with any attempt to change, the success of this will depend on the man's willingness to take responsibility. The skill of the counsellor in identifying the issue of abuse, and challenging the man about it, is vital.

The decision to have joint or individual counselling will depend on your situation. In deciding consider the following questions:

- Will I feel safe enough to disclose the ways my partner is abusing me and how this is affecting me, with him present?
- Will I be strong enough outside the counsellor's office to cope with my partner's possible negative reactions to my honesty?
- Do I fear my partner's emotional or physical retaliation? Could speaking out in a counselling session put my safety at risk?

Couples counselling is not recommended if you are afraid of your partner's reactions to your honest participation. If your self-esteem and confidence are at a low ebb, it is usually better to work individually with a counsellor initially, and then move into joint sessions when you are ready. In joint counselling the woman sometimes finds that because she is in a highly emotional and anxious state, and her partner presents as a caring and charming man, the counsellor gains a false impression of what is happening within the relationship. This can mean the woman does not receive the validation and support she is entitled to. If you do decide to attend counselling with your partner, be sure to evaluate the counsellor's performance using the criteria listed on page 107. Don't be afraid to terminate joint counselling if you feel it is not meeting your needs.

The most powerful thing I realised was that if I chose to act differently, then it broke the usual pattern of behaviour and Mark was forced to come at it from a different angle. If there was a hassle I'd say, 'I'm not getting into this now', and I'd go out for a walk instead of arguing. A change was almost forced, because the reaction he used to fight against wasn't there any more.

Get clear on your boundaries

In deciding to reclaim your equality within the relationship, one of the most important concepts to understand and work with is that of personal boundaries. A boundary is the invisible line around each of us which separates us from other people. Inside that protective boundary is everything that is important to our individuality, including our beliefs, opinions, feelings, rights and needs. Personal boundaries define how close we allow a person to come, and how much of ourselves we are willing to give. Controlling men do not respect boundaries; they invade them.

In an equal relationship, both partners have clear boundaries which are flexible yet firm enough to maintain healthy individuality. Both partners decide for themselves where they stand on various issues and what interactions are acceptable to them. In a controlling relationship, one partner refuses to respect the rights of the other to be separate and self-determining. Our attempts at setting limits are often ignored.

I never realised it at the time, but right from the beginning Tony violated my boundaries in all kinds of ways. He was so full-on, I was just swept along. He wouldn't take 'No' for an answer. He'd talk non-stop and expect me to give him my undivided attention. He'd quizz me about my childhood and get right into analysing it. He even dissected and debated my spirituality. He'd want sex constantly, and would keep me awake half the night. After a while I felt as if I'd been turned inside out. Sometimes I'd feel a surge of anger and want to push him away, but then I'd tell myself I was being unreasonable and that he meant well.

Our uncomfortable feelings and physical reactions are the natural warning signals which tell us when our boundaries are being violated. Most of us are so out of touch with our internal responses, we are unaware of the significance of these signals. A knot in the stomach or feeling of agitation often go unnoticed or are not recognised for the signals they are.

In our increasing confusion, we may also be unclear where our limits lie. This is especially true for those of us who have had our boundaries violated by abuse when we were children. Those early violations can leave us feeling that we don't have the right to boundaries that define our own separate self. We may be unaware when our partner is invading our boundaries because we are unsure of where they are or where they should be. We may also feel apprehensive about setting and enforcing limits that protect us, because it was not possible to do so when we were children.

Exercise: Recognise boundary invasions

One of the most important ways we can reclaim our equality is by learning to recognise when our boundaries are being violated. Being brow-beaten and bullied into giving way on issues that involve personal rights is boundary invasion. Think of a time recently when you tried unsuccessfully to say 'No' to your partner. Explore this situation by asking yourself the following questions:

- How was I feeling? Was my body giving me any signals that my boundaries were being violated?
- What (if anything) could I have done differently, so that the situation would have resulted in a better outcome for me?
- Do I believe I have the right to claim this boundary for myself, or am I unsure of my ground?

Acknowledge your rights

To reclaim our equality in the relationship, it is vital that we begin to regain a sense of being a separate person with individual rights. When we live with a controlling man, it is very easy to lose sight of this. But if we are clear about our entitlement to our rights, we are in a far stronger position to achieve them. As we reclaim our rights, we are pushing our boundaries back into place. The following list will remind you of your basic human rights.

As people we are entitled to . . .
- be treated with respect;
- have our own separate, independent identity;
- have our needs for appreciation, affection and support met;
- change our mind, make mistakes and fail;
- make decisions about our own lives;
- say 'no' when we want to;
- have and express all our feelings, thoughts and opinions;
- have privacy and solitude, and our own secrets;
- spend time with the people we choose;
- pursue our own interests and goals;
- have the time and freedom to do what makes us happy;
- live a life which is free of harassment.

Exercise: Naming your 'lost' rights

Your freedom may have been eroded so far that you are not sure if you have any rights. Acknowledging this is the first step in change. Put a mark beside the rights you are not able to claim at the moment. Reflect on, or write about, the impact this has on your self-esteem, lifestyle and well-being. This may prompt you to add extra goals to the list suggested on p. 155. Reclaiming your rights can be a slow process that takes careful planning and small steps, but it is possible to do it.

Recognise the games that are played

Many controlling men are skilful at manipulating their partners into a 'one-down' position. Even though the same patterns or games may be played repeatedly to achieve this, the games may be so subtle that we fail to recognise them. Without knowing it, we can slide into responding to certain recurring situations in ways that leave us feeling short-changed.

Every now and again I'd wake up to something that Vince was doing and I'd name it. Like one time he was bickering with me and getting nasty, and suddenly it just really came clear to me that this was a pattern where he'd denigrate me until I was feeling really horrible, and afterward he'd come to me and I'd be so desperately grateful that he wasn't mad at me any more that we'd make love. I can remember suddenly turning round one time and saying to him, 'Is this the let's put Donna down and make her miserable so we can have sex game?' He just stopped with his mouth open and looked really shocked. Looking back, that was quite a little turning point in the relationship. He couldn't play that game again, because both of us now knew it.

Because our partner knows our vulnerabilities, he knows the issues on which we will try to defend ourselves. He often plays on these points, sometimes without even being consciously aware he is doing it. Before we can protect ourselves from this, we need to be aware of what is happening.

Exercise: Identifying a recurring game

Think of an area of conflict with your partner in which a repeating pattern of events occurs. Explore this situation, preferably in writing, using the following questions as a guide:

- How did the conflict begin?
- What did my partner say and do?
- Did my partner use a particular tactic to hook me in?
- What did I say and do?
- Is this the way the 'scene' is usually played?
- Did he have a hidden agenda? What pay-off did he get from the game?
- Was there any pay-off for me?

Refusing to play the game

Once we are aware of the ways our partner is setting us up and pulling the strings, we can refuse to dance to his tune.

Frank had a back problem which supposedly gave him a lot of pain. He'd be bent double every morning, and I hated to see him like that, so I'd give him a massage. Trouble was, it never seemed to get any better; in fact the groans of pain got louder if I missed a day. After a while I started to find it quite a pressure giving him a massage in the morning when I was rushing for work. Then we went away with some friends for a few days and there was no sore back! I couldn't believe it. I realised he'd been playing on my sympathy all that time, and I was so angry that he could have been so selfish. That was the last morning massage he ever got. At first the groans got even louder, but I just ignored them. Then miraculously after a couple of weeks they disappeared and that was the end of the sore back.

Exercise: Choosing different moves

To change our behaviour successfully we need to have thought through the possibilities carefully, decided on a new course of action and prepared ourselves mentally and emotionally. Referring to the 'game' you have identified above, think about a number of alternative scenarios that could have resulted if you had played your part differently.

Possible strategies for changing a pattern include:

- Do the opposite of what you always do.
- Refuse by your actions to play your part, without directly confronting your partner's behaviour.
- Directly name the 'game' and point out the roles you each play.
- Openly refuse to play.

When you have mentally explored the various options, choose one strategy to use the next time your partner initiates this particular game.

Taking a stand

The most important skill we can learn when dealing with our controlling partner is that of setting limits. By setting a limit, we define what we want and what we are not willing to tolerate. In effect we are saying, 'This far and no further.'

Ideally this is backed up by an action that reinforces this boundary.

> After I decided to set limits, Alan would say something to initiate an argument and I'd make a clear statement like, 'I do not want to argue, I will not be involved in this, and I'm not talking about it any more', and that was that. Then I'd remove myself from the house if necessary. It was hard at first, because it was the opposite to what I'd always done and I didn't know what his reactions would be. But it did get easier.

'No' can be the most difficult, yet effective, word to say to a controlling man. Reclaiming our power on long-standing issues and getting to the bottom-line message of 'No' has often to be done in stages.

> Sex first became an issue when Jim wanted sex after our first child was born. I wasn't ready, and Jim threatened to go elsewhere. Of course I gave in. From then it became an on-going problem that was supposedly all mine. It has taken me a long time to get over my sense of power-lessness and be able to set limits. Before I could do this, I affirmed my sexuality by reading books and going to courses. Once I realised it was not my problem if I didn't want sex as often as he did, I felt more confident. The first tiny boundary I set with sex was to insist we use lubrication. Then I'd sometimes say, 'It's still hurting', in the hope he would respect me enough to stop. Sometimes he did, but often he'd just go on anyway. So I gradually began to say 'No' if I didn't want sex. Now I am careful to stay tuned into what I really want, and to work at being true to that. The relationship has improved a lot as I've become more sure of myself.

Before we set a limit on what we are willing to tolerate, it is best to work out what we will do if our partner refuses to respect that limit. Then if he does refuse, we can follow a clear course of action that shows our partner we will no longer be manipulated.

> Mark was often unreliable. He'd say he'd take us out somewhere and just not turn up. Not only did I have to

deal with my own anger about it, but I'd have to pacify the kids as well. He wouldn't take any notice of what I said about it, so in the end I made a decision that I'd have to carry on on my own and not rely on him. After that, if I had to be somewhere at a certain time and he hadn't turned up, I'd go. He got a bit more punctual then.

Doing things differently in the relationship is likely to make us feel extremely anxious, especially if our partner's response is anger. Many of us are so distressed by anger we will do anything to avoid it, but if we are committed to challenging the status quo it will be necessary to practise standing firm despite our fears. While doing this it can help to remind ourselves that we are not responsible for our partner's feelings. It is his choice to get angry. We don't need to work to pacify him.

When Barry gets angry at me I've developed several ways of handling it. Sometimes I simply acknowledge his feelings by saying something like, 'I can see you're really upset', without taking responsibility for that or feeling that I need to fix it. Or I might just say, 'If you don't stop shouting, I'm going to leave the room', and then follow that through. Sometimes I'll raise my voice to match his and say things like, 'I don't want to hear what you think is wrong with me. I'm quite capable of telling you what I think and feel. I'm willing to listen to what your feelings are, and what you think about yourself.' That often takes the wind out of his sails and he'll calm down.

Be aware that some men will resort to violence to regain control if their partner begins to set limits. *Be careful! In some relationships it is impossible to set limits and stay safe.* In this situation the only safe limit we can set is to leave.

Strategies for setting limits

- Decide on the limit you will set on a particular issue ahead of time. Be clear about your right to set that limit.

- Plan what you will say, and practise this with a support group, counsellor or friend.
- When you set the limit, make the statement as directly as possible, without apology or justification.
- Be prepared for your partner's reaction. Don't get drawn into his communication games. (See 'Communication games', p. 167.)
- Don't get hooked into debating reasons. Use the 'broken record' technique of simply repeating your limit-setting statement.
- Decide beforehand what action you will take if your partner refuses to respect your boundaries. Follow through if necessary.
- Consider giving your partner an either/or alternative ahead of time so that he is clear what the consequence will be if he continues his unacceptable behaviour. Name only the consequences you can realistically carry out.
- Be consistent about enforcing your limits. You may need to assess these periodically, to make sure the limits you have set are still appropriate for you.

Exercise: Setting your limits

Think of an area of the relationship in which you feel that your rights or needs are being violated. This could be about freedom, money, sex, privacy or self-expression. Ask yourself:

- How does this violation make me feel?
- What is most important to me in this situation? What do and don't I want?
- Do I have a clear boundary on this issue?
- Is this boundary a true reflection of what is right for me?
- What is really acceptable to me in this situation?
- What new boundary would I like to set?
- What will I do if my partner refuses to respect my limit?

Don't sabotage yourself

Standing our ground when there is conflict can be frightening. In the heat of the moment we can unconsciously undermine ourselves in many ways. Sometimes we give ourselves self-defeating messages like, 'He's not going to let me get away with this', or, 'I'm too weak to stand up to him.' It is important to make a conscious effort to notice when we are giving ourselves undermining messages, and to stop doing it.

In the midst of conflict we may also lose touch with our own internal responses. We over-identify with our partner's moods, words and actions instead of maintaining an awareness of how we are feeling and what is right for us.

To stay in our own power during conflict, we need to develop the ability to stand back mentally and to focus on our truth. When you are involved in conflict, develop the habit of asking yourself the following questions:

- How am I really feeling about what's happening here?
- What am I telling myself about it?
- What is right for me in this situation?
- How can I act in a way that protects and strengthens me?

When we know how we feel and what we want, we can use this as the basis of action. We are able to choose our responses, so that we become proactive instead of reactive.

Communication games

Most of us find it extremely difficult to live with a man who refuses to communicate. Many controlling men are masters at playing communication games which leave their partners feeling completely frustrated and unheard.

> Whenever I tried to discuss any issue with John he'd do everything in his power to stop me. He'd tell me my timing was wrong, or he'd talk me down or flip the subject around and go off on a side issue. Often he'd accuse me of making a big deal out of things. He'd tell me not to be so stupid, that I was imagining things. Sometimes he'd even laugh in my face when I was upset, which was really distressing. His favourite was to tell me it was all my problem and I needed professional help. He didn't have a problem. It was so infuriating, it almost drove me crazy.

It is easy to fall into the habit of making all the attempts at communication while our partner continues to block our efforts. Often the most empowering approach to our partner's games is to back off and stop trying. This change in our behaviour can result in our partner also changing his position.

Strategies for dealing with communication games

- Make a point of recognising when your partner is playing games, and stand back from them.
- Give up trying to discuss issues rationally when he is being irrational.
- Refuse to be drawn into no-win discussions.
- When you want to get a point across, mentally prepare what you want to say. State your point briefly and refuse to get drawn into an argument about it.
- Don't get hooked into explaining, justifying, arguing, clarifying or apologising to your partner when he is playing games.
- If your partner criticises you, don't waste your energy trying to convince him he is wrong about you. Tell yourself, 'What he thinks of me is none of my business.'

Dealing with wounding words

We do not need our partner's criticism, put-downs or blame, so it is essential that we learn to deflect, sidestep and reject it. As we begin to accept that his harsh criticism has nothing to do with us, we are taking a big step in regaining our power.

> An incredible breakthrough came for me when I realised I didn't have to take on what anyone else said. When Chris said something that was unkind or hurtful to me, it still only belonged to him. It didn't involve me at all. I used to own everything he said and none of it actually belonged to me. This realisation really blew my mind.

Having decided not to accept your partner's criticisms, there are several ways you can deal with them. You may need to experiment to discover which suggestions you feel comfortable with and which work best in your situation.

Dealing with criticism that attacks your self-image

No one has the right to attack our self-image, but abusive men frequently do. Learn to listen for and reject criticism that begins: 'You're . . .' and is followed by your partner's judgement of the moment: 'stupid', 'demanding', 'a bad mother', 'a liar', 'selfish', 'lazy', 'fat', 'ugly', 'crazy', and so on.

Your partner is not entitled to judge you in these ways. Refuse to wear these labels. Remind yourself that they say more about your partner's ability to be cutting and cruel than they do about your worth.

Think about the ways you deal with these verbal assaults. If your usual direct protest leads to further abuse, try something different. It is important not to accept these criticisms. Sometimes it is enough simply to acknowledge to yourself that the criticism is incorrect. Alternatively you may want to tell your partner in a short, clear statement that you will not accept what he is saying.

Dealing with exaggerated criticism

Sometimes our partner's criticism may contain a small grain of truth but the facts are wildly exaggerated. That grain of truth can hook us into accepting our partner's criticism unreservedly.

Develop the habit of noticing when your partner uses the words 'always' or 'never' in his criticism. You may choose to diffuse these criticisms by putting the record straight. For example:

Exaggerated criticism: 'You never want sex.'
Possible response: 'No, that's not true. Tonight I don't want sex, but often I do.'

Exaggerated criticism: 'You're always out doing your own thing these days.'
Possible response: 'No, that's an exaggeration. I only go out two nights a week.'

The controlling man often does his best to make us feel guilty if we in any way assert our rights or needs. We don't need to feel guilty for not being constantly available to our partner. We are entitled to care for ourselves and to be less than perfect. We do not need to measure up to the standards our partner tries to impose.

Dealing with unjust criticism

It is really important we don't accept criticism that is untrue. Try rejecting such an attack with a short statement that gives the clear message that you do not accept it.

> After I decided not to take Keith's criticism on board any more, things definitely improved. Whenever he'd start on me, I'd say in a dead-pan voice, 'That's your opinion but I don't agree', or 'You've told me that before.' I just refused to buy into it any more, and he knew it. Once he realised his criticism wasn't having the desired effect, he stopped a lot of it. Before that I used to try to defend myself verbally, but that was hopeless. He'd get right into it and things would get really nasty.

When challenging your partner's criticism, keep your message simple and direct. If your partner is being unreasonable, he will not listen to your explanations anyway. Justifications often just provide him with new issues to pick up on and use against you.

Possible responses to unjustified criticism include:
- 'I disagree.'
- 'It's wrong when you say that.'
- 'My point of view is very different from yours.'
- 'It didn't happen that way.'
- 'I feel hurt when you accuse me unjustly.'
- 'I'm not willing to accept your criticism.'
- 'I resent that statement.'
- 'I find that insulting.'

If it is too threatening to make a clear statement to your partner, then at least make the statement to yourself. This helps to shield you from the impact of his words.

Visualisation exercise: Shield yourself

Each time your partner subjects you to a verbal attack, keep the thought in your mind that you do not deserve it. You are a worthwhile person. You do not need to accept what he says.

Imagine you have an invisible, protective shield around you. Your partner's harsh words can no longer reach you. Imagine them just hitting the shield, bouncing off and falling to the ground without hurting you. (See also 'Taking a stand', p. 163.)

Taking stock

Regaining our power in a controlling relationship requires an ongoing commitment and the determination to make a consistent effort to resist our partner's control tactics. As we do this there may be positive changes in the way our partner treats us, but in relating in this way there will also be losses. Having constantly to stand back and set limits does not leave us much room to get our need for closeness met. If it is frequently necessary to protect ourselves from our partner's destructive behaviour, it is not possible to develop the intimacy and trust that makes a relationship deeply fulfilling.

When a relationship is changing, whether this is because you, or your partner, have initiated change, it is useful to stand back on a regular basis and evaluate what is taking place.

Exercise: Measuring your partner's change

Because one form of abuse may be replaced by another, it is important to look at the overall pattern of control. Complete the following checklist either weekly, fortnightly or monthly, so you can have a clear measure of your situation.

See diagram over page.

During the last ___ week(s) my partner has . . . 1: *Never* 2: *Occasionally* 3: *Frequently*	Week/Fortnight/Month			
	1	2	3	4
Treated me with disrespect				
Given me the silent treatment				
Used punishing behaviour				
Denied or twisted the truth				
Called me names or unfairly criticised me				
Deprived me of sleep				
Restricted my contact with others				
Sabotaged my plans				
Shown excessive jealousy				
Refused to consult me on important decisions				
Unfairly withheld money				
Undermined my position with the children				
Treated me like a servant				
Insisted I have sex when I didn't want it				
Used standover tactics				
Intimidated me with anger				
Destroyed property				
Threatened to hurt people, myself included				
Been in any way physically abusive: including restraining, spitting, throwing objects, pushing, slapping or punching.				

Weighing the cost against the gains

We use a great deal of energy in working to reclaim our power, so we need to be mindful of the cost of our efforts, as well as the pleasure of the harmonious times.

> I've stayed in the relationship because there are some positives there. Most of the time we are reasonably happy now. The controlling behaviour is still there, although much less than before. As one type of abuse stops, a new one often emerges. I realise that at some level John has a need to be abusive, and that need will

probably always be there. That'll only change if he wants it to. I see that there is a continuing cycle that will probably keep recurring. I've developed strategies for dealing with it but I often have to ask myself, 'Why stay? Is it worth it?' Each time the cycle comes around, I have to make the choice again. Realistically I know that when I choose to stay living in this situation, that's what I'm choosing.

Exercise: Re-evaluating your situation

When you have worked at reclaiming your power for a time, consider the following questions:

- How many of my goals for personal change have I been able to achieve?
- What impact has this had on the way my partner treats me? As I've reclaimed my power, has his behaviour changed for better or worse? Has he shown he is capable of respecting my limits?
- What has the personal cost of these changes been?
- Am I gaining enough out of this relationship to make it worthwhile?

The effort required to claim equality may be on-going, but for some women it is well worth it. As they continue to strengthen themselves, their relationship gradually improves.

The challenge is to keep growing in spite of it all; not to give up, but at the same time not to give in. I'm finding it easier all the time to stop and think before I say anything, and not to panic when I start to feel intimidated. I have learned to maintain an even keel and not to stop asserting myself when Kim wants me to, but just to keep going. Now I'm at the stage where I can say, 'I need this', or 'I'm doing that, and I'm doing it at my own pace.' As I've got stronger, there have been huge changes in the relationship. It used to take weeks for the things I said to get through to Kim. Now it might take just an hour. Most of the time I'm being met with respect now. What I have learned is to be my own person within the relationship, and look at what I want and need. I've had to regain my power the hard way, by saying 'No' very strongly. It is an ongoing challenge, but it can be done, and in my case it has been worth it.

This chapter has offered a number of suggestions for gradually reclaiming equality within your relationship. In developing an ability to protect yourself by setting limits on what you will not accept, you will gradually regain your power, your self-respect and self-trust. The success of this approach in creating positive changes within the relationship will ultimately depend on your partner's willingness to behave more reasonably. If he is determined to crush you into submission with his punishing tactics, he could make your life increasingly miserable. Never allow yourself to forget that you have the right and the power to choose again about your future. You are entitled to an unrestricted, fulfilling life.

Chapter Eleven

The Challenge of Breaking Free

A journey of a thousand miles begins with one step

– from *The Simple Way*, Lao Tszi

For many of us there comes a time when there is nothing left to cushion us from reality. Our dreams have turned to dust, our efforts have proved to be in vain, and our love has been lost into a void. We have tried to make positive changes, turned the other cheek, hoped against hope and prayed for a miracle. Now we realise that no matter what the cost, we have to pick up the broken pieces of our lives and go on alone. What once meant the world to us is no more.

It takes so much courage to take that one crucial step into an unknown future. But it is amazing how, when the time is right, we find that inner strength to move. This chapter will guide you as you take the steps leading to the break-up of your relationship and out into a new life.

Preparing for the break-up

Before we embark on any journey we usually make preparations. This journey is no exception. In fact the more prepared we are, the better we fare. It is important to anticipate and plan for the challenges we will encounter so that they don't catch us unaware.

Generally, if we intend to leave, the sooner we do it the better. Starting again never gets easier as we get older. Sometimes there seem to be good reasons to postpone the move. The children may be completing their schooling or we may be looking for employment or trying to save money.

The trouble is, one reason can give way to another. If we are not careful, these reasons can continue to hold us prisoner for years. Some women end up postponing the separation until their physical or mental health breaks down. This makes it much harder. Others stay until they are literally forced to flee, under attack, into the night. Some of these women return to their partners because they were not prepared for the break-up at that time.

Preparation happens on several levels: emotional, practical and mental.

Emotional preparation: Facing fears

Breaking up requires that we take a leap into the unknown. As we consider the end of the relationship, we are usually tormented by fears. How will I manage on my own? Am I strong enough to cope? What if I end up alone for ever? Am I making a dreadful mistake I will live to regret?

It is normal to be terrified of leaving a relationship. It is a huge step. Our lives will never be the same again, although almost certainly they will change for the better. Most of us try to cope with our fears by ignoring them. But the more we deny them, the more they persist. Unacknowledged fears play on our minds and sap our confidence until we have no energy left to deal with the problems at hand.

The way out of fear is through it. To conquer our fears we need to step boldly into them. This involves the same process we use for dealing with all feelings: *awareness*, *acknowledgement* and *acceptance*. When we become aware of our fears and acknowledge them fully, we begin to accept them as valid expressions of who we are.

As we face and feel our vulnerability, our fear may increase in intensity for a brief time. Then it begins to diminish. When we know what we are dealing with, much of the power of that feeling goes. We move through fear to a calmer, stronger place within. Having faced the worst, we are free to put our energy into coping creatively with our situation.

> Before the break-up the fear was really crippling. But once I took that one step into my fear it was amazing,

because the fear was just like a mist and it didn't seem to matter any more. I found it was actually okay, and that was such a relief.

Exercise: Acknowledging and redefining your fears

By putting our fears on paper we give them a face and reduce them to specific issues. This is the first and most important step in overcoming them. To clarify your fears, head a sheet of paper: 'When I think about leaving, I'm afraid that . . .' Now write a full list of all your fears, large and small, including those you believe are irrational or insignificant.

When we are afraid, our minds usually create the worst possible scenarios. We tend to think in very black and white terms, and the words we use to describe our fears often reflect this. Using words like 'can't', 'never', 'will', 'won't', 'all', 'everyone', 'no one', 'nowhere' to define our problems can make them seem insoluble.

Go through your list and underline all these exaggerated words. For example:

- 'I <u>will</u> be all alone.'
- 'I <u>can't</u> go. I'm just too scared.'
- 'We just <u>won't</u> be able to survive on a benefit.'
- '<u>Everyone</u> thinks I should stay.'
- 'I have <u>nowhere</u> to go.'

Now rewrite the first of your statements in a more general and open way. Substitute the exaggerated words you have underlined for ones that allow options, like 'could', 'can', 'may not', 'may', 'sometimes', 'some people', and so on.

Next use the word *but* to lead you into stating broader possibilities in the second half of the sentence.

Follow this process for each statement. For example:

- 'I may be alone sometimes *but* I will be free to seek company when I want to.'
- 'It is natural to feel afraid of leaving *but* that doesn't need to stop me. I can overcome my fears.'
- 'We may find it difficult to manage on less money *but* we will cope somehow.'

- 'Some people think I should stay *but* they have no way of knowing how bad this is for me.'
- 'I'm not sure where I'll go *but* I can begin to find out the various options.'

Rewriting in this way immediately broadens the possibilities and redefines our fears into specific problems. This is progress, because where there is a problem there is also a solution.

Exercise: Create a bottom line

Acknowledging our worst fear, and having a strategy to deal with it, helps us to feel stronger and more in control. Try asking yourself the following questions:

- If I imagine my life after the break-up, what would be the worst possible outcome?
- If this should happen, what would I do?

You have probably pictured a desperate situation, so you may wish to choose a very bold and desperate solution. It is unlikely you will need to act on it, but when you have this plan of action you know that no matter what happens you can, and will, cope. From this strong stance you can face the future with more confidence.

Practical preparation: Tackling problems

Where there is a will there is a way. There are always far more solutions to a problem than there at first seem. The challenge is to open our minds wide enough to discover what they are.

The way we define a problem has a direct impact on our ability to resolve it. If we state our problem in a fixed way, it can seem like an insurmountable barrier. However, when we state that problem as a question, we invite a solution. For example, stating, 'We have nowhere to go if we leave' creates a brick wall, whereas the question, 'Where can we go if we leave?' opens the door for an answer. As we ask our question, we are also asking our creative mind to explore possibilities and find solutions.

Overcoming problems can be a mind-boggling task, but if it is broken down into steps it becomes manageable. What do you consider your greatest problem in leaving the relationship? Try tackling this problem in the following way:

Exercise: Taking steps to solve problems

1. State the problem as a question.
2. List all the possible courses of action, no matter how trivial or unlikely they seem. (At this stage, the more possibilities on your list the better, as this helps to make you feel less restricted.)
3. Gather new information. (By bouncing your question off others and seeking new facts, you can discover possibilities that you weren't aware of. This extends your range of options.) Add the new possibilities to your list.
4. Consider each of the options on your list separately. What are the benefits and drawbacks of each?
5. Eliminate any options that are clearly unsuitable.
6. Choose the best option.
7. List the steps involved in actioning your choice. What is the first step you will take?
8. Last, but most important: take that first step.

The first steps of change are usually the hardest. We may not be quite sure of where we are going, but as we take each step the path will gradually become clearer.

Mental preparation: Creating a positive future

Without even being aware of it, many of us hold an extremely negative view of our future. We unconsciously picture and speak about the worst possible outcomes. This can constantly undermine our confidence and keep us paralysed with fear. In a sense, we are being held a prisoner by our own imagination.

> The build-up to leaving was terrible. I was terrified of living alone. I imagined that it'd be absolutely awful. That the silence was going to close in on me and engulf me. That I'd become so depressed, I wouldn't be able to get out of bed. That no one would care what happened to me. I thought I'd just be left totally isolated.

Our imagination is a powerful force. We can choose to use our mind to pave our way to freedom.

Visualisation exercise: Picture your future

First spend a few minutes thinking about the way you usually picture your future.
- How do you imagine life after the break-up is going to be?
- What do you see yourself doing?
- What are you telling yourself?
- How does this make you feel?

Now spend some time using your mind to rewrite the script.
- If it were possible to have your life as you want it after the break-up, how would it be?
- What do you see yourself doing in your imaginary new life?
- What are you telling yourself?
- How does this make you feel?

The second part of this exercise may require practice. We are not accustomed to visualising a very different life from the one we have been accustomed to. At first the thought of having the life we want can seem an impossibility. But the more time we spend consciously visualising this positive life, the more believable it becomes. In using your imagination in this way you are creating a powerful blueprint for the future. Eventually the way of life that you began to picture as an impossible dream can become a new reality.

Exercise: Affirm your decision

The messages we give ourselves are crucial. Make a point of noticing when you are telling yourself something that makes you feel afraid. Stop that thought and soothe your fears with affirmations. Either make up some that are meaningful to you, or try these:
- I deserve peace and happiness.
- I have the right to be free.
- I am strong enough to stand alone.

- I have the power to create a secure and happy life for myself.
- I am open to receiving the support I need.
- I have enough strength to meet any challenges.
- Everything is working out for the best.
- Positive changes are now occurring in my life.

Every time you give yourself an affirmation, you are building your inner strength and opening yourself up to the reality of a positive future.

Strategies for preparing to break up

- Find out all the information you can on useful community resources and if necessary housing options.
- If you intend to go on a benefit, find out the procedure and criteria for applying. Find out if you are entitled to any other type of assistance.
- Begin to put aside as much money as you can.
- Make a plan of what you will do and where you will go. Rehearse the steps of the plan in your mind in a positive way.
- If you are finding it difficult to plan for the break-up by yourself, work on this with a friend or counsellor.
- Decide who you need help from, and arrange it with them.

Should I tell my partner I'm leaving?

Deciding whether to tell your partner you are leaving is an individual choice. If there is any possibility of his trying to stop you or becoming violent, it is best not to do so. As the following woman's experience shows, it can be difficult to predict how your partner may react. Confrontations can end in unexpected crisis.

> I found Mike with another woman just three days after he had showered me with roses and taken me out for a special wedding anniversary dinner. After that wonderful evening, it was too much. I'd had enough and I told him that was it. He went into a real rage and got me around the neck and started squeezing. He actually

lifted me right off the floor. I really thought he was going to kill me. He'd never been violent before, and I hadn't even realised he had it in him, but he'd totally lost it. Then he let me go and went outside. I was so terrified, I locked him out. Our four-year-old daughter was there, and she was upset and went to let her Daddy in. That's when he broke the door down. It came right down on top of her and knocked her out. I thought he'd killed her and it really broke me.

Rather than take the risk of telling your partner ahead of time, it may be advisable just to leave and contact him later.

Gaining other people's support

The support of the people who love you can literally be a life-saver. If you have reached the point where you are too demoralised and exhausted to make the move alone, you need to tell other people, loud and clear, just how desperate you are. You need to find someone you can trust to help you. (See 'Choosing a confidant', p. 97.) Tell that person how crucial it is for your health and safety that you leave and ask for their help. If the first person you approach does not understand your dilemma, or is unwilling to help you, then find someone else who will. Whatever you do, don't give up.

Sometimes family are not the best people to ask for support. They may think they know better than you how to live your life and not mind telling you so. Sometimes they have their own personal reasons for giving you the advice they do, and although well-meaning, this advice can be totally wrong for you.

Mum put a lot of pressure on me to go back. She said Bill really loved the kids. She said I'd always had problems and been depressed, and would still have problems regardless of whether I left Bill. Afterwards I sat outside and drank a whole bottle of wine and the tears were just rolling down my face. I thought it was hopeless and I'd have to go back, and I did. But I had to go to the doctor's first and get anti-depressants. I just couldn't have gone back to him otherwise. The next time I didn't let anyone stop me.

Other people's control and criticism reinforces your partner's abuse and further undermines you. Do not let anyone convince you to stay against your own judgement. Find people who will support you in following your inner wisdom. Only you know the pain you are living in and understand the desperation of your situation. You need support from someone who is willing to walk alongside you as you find your own way, not someone who will take over your life.

The role of Women's Aid

One of the best sources of expert information, advice and help is Women's Aid. They offer nationwide support to women who are in emotionally or physically abusive relationships. They provide a 24-hour phone service and advice on safe confidential houses for women and their children to stay in if they need to leave their home because they are afraid of a partner. Transport to the house can be arranged if necessary. Don't be afraid to reach out for their support. The women who provide the service are there because they care. (See the list of resources, pp. 244–58 for contact phone numbers).

How will my partner react?

Your ending the relationship represents the ultimate threat to your partner's control. As the woman's experience on p. 181 shows, it is impossible for you to predict exactly how he will react. It is, however, fairly safe to assume that he will attempt to change your mind both before and after the separation. For the sake of your own survival, you may need to harden your heart and put up barriers against your partner's pleas or aggression. This will help you to weather the storm while remaining firm in your resolve to separate.

As he realises you are serious about separation, your partner is likely to try a variety of tactics to bring you around. These may include remorse, promises, playing on your fears, finding another woman, threats of suicide, intimidation or threats of violence. Remember that his behaviour may become extreme. His initial charm and reassurances may turn alarmingly to intimidation and threats. Always put your safety first and don't take any risks.

Remorse and promises

When your partner first realises you want out, it is likely that he will become remorseful. He may turn on his charm and tell you how much he loves you, swear the abuse will never happen again and beg you to reconsider. When these are the words you've been longing to hear, it is tempting to believe them.

Because they take us by surprise, many of us are drawn back by words like these. We tell ourselves that maybe this time our partner has learned his lesson and has reached that turning point where he will make some positive changes. Sadly, these pleas often turn out to be just another control tactic.

> I actually found myself a flat and rang to tell him, and he just started to cry and cry. He begged me to come back. He said he was so sorry and he'd do anything if I would, so I weakened and went back. But nothing really changed, and in six months I left again for the final time. I was in even worse shape by then.

Occasionally, in the heat of the moment, our partners may stop blaming us long enough to admit that they have a problem themselves. Generally they define this problem as 'anger', 'poor communication', 'stress', 'alcohol' or 'drugs'. Rarely do abusive men define their problem as an overriding need for control. When faced with the prospect of losing their partner, some men agree to work on their 'problem' through self-restraint, effort, counselling or attending a programme. Unfortunately their promises often don't progress past their rash words; once the critical moment has passed, and we have agreed to stay, action is easily postponed. If your partner is serious about seeking help, there are various options available. (See 'If your partner is willing to get help', p. 156.) If your partner does begin to work at making changes, it is a good idea to keep a record of progress by using the checklist on p. 172.

It takes sincere hard work and commitment to change. If your partner promises to work on his behaviour, you need to ask yourself how likely this really is.

- Does he truly believe he has a problem, or is he just trying to win you round?
- Has he made promises and broken them before?

Rather than staying on the basis of a rash promise, it is often better to proceed with your plans. If your partner really is committed to change, the possibility of losing you permanently may be just the incentive he needs.

Playing on our fears

Murray used to say to me, 'Who the devil would want you with three kids?' That upset me because I didn't want to be alone. I'd watch old ladies on the beach picking up glass, and I'd think, 'That's going to be me. There's not going to be anyone there for me.' That kept me in the relationship for a long time. Little did I know that I'd meet my second husband almost immediately after the break-up and go on to have a really good second marriage, full of love and trust.

Controlling men would have us believe that we cannot manage without them. They are in for a surprise. Once we have gone through the transition and rebuilt our self-esteem, anything is possible. Life without our abusive partner can be as enjoyable and interesting as we decide to make it. (See 'The ways women healed their wounds,' p. 217.)

Finding another woman

After the break-up, some men react by replacing us almost immediately with another woman. For a few women this is a relief, because it takes the pressure off us. For many, however, it is the final shattering betrayal. Having poured heart and soul into our relationship for so long, it makes a mockery of all our effort and pain.

We'd all been away on the boat, and Nigel was so awful to my girls. He kept calling them thick, dumb and stupid

– two little girls who weren't very old. I told him I'd had
enough and asked him to take us back home. When he
dropped us off, he was still ranting and raving, real nasty.
Then the next thing I heard him on the phone, voice
all soft, doing his Mr Nice Guy act, talking to the woman
he had been going out with three years ago before I'd
come on the scene. He was asking her if she wanted to
come away with him on his boat. I couldn't believe it.
After all I'd been through. I packed and moved out that
day and he's been with her ever since.

When we see our partner on his best behaviour with a new
woman, we can be reduced to doubting ourselves again. Was
his bad behaviour our own fault, after all? We forget that this
new relationship will have a honeymoon period, just as ours
did. In many cases, time proves that our ex-partner has not
changed. We watch as the new woman succumbs to his
charm, only to find herself enmeshed in a similar trap to the
one we have escaped. Ironically, some of these women may
later approach us for help to deal with that same abusive man.

Threat of suicide

When your partner threatens suicide, you are placed in a real
dilemma. Does he mean what he says? Dare I risk it? How
could I live with myself if he did it? Some women remain
trapped for years, risking their own safety and sanity because
of their fear that their partner will take his own life.

I couldn't stand it any more. I knew I was going to die if
I stayed. When I told Wayne I was leaving, he got really
angry and shouted at me and then he stormed out of
the house. After a few minutes I heard a scream and went
out and he was hanging by a rope around his neck, but
he was holding onto it with his hand. He must have let
himself down onto it and it had pulled on his neck, and
then he'd yelled. That's how I saw him. I rushed to the
phone and rang a neighbour, and when I got back he'd
got himself down. Although he had threatened to kill
himself several times before that, he never mentioned
it again.

There is no way of knowing if your partner is seriously considering suicide or if he is just trying to manipulate you into staying. The threat of suicide should therefore always be taken seriously. This does not mean, however, that you must stay. No woman can be expected to stay on in a destructive relationship in an effort to ensure her partner's survival. What you can do is reduce the risk by telling your partner's friends and family of his threats. Ask them to support him after the break-up. Give your partner the phone numbers of a crisis phone line, hospital (mental health unit) and a counsellor, and encourage him to reach out for support. Ultimately he is responsible for his own choices.

Intimidation or threats of violence

> I moved to another town and had been there for three months when all of a sudden Des just arrived at my door. It really blew me away. I got such a shock, I went straight back into helpless panic and let him in, even though I shouldn't have. Later that night I was in his car, and I just remember all this verbal abuse coming at me, and I was crying and screaming. I felt so uptight I wanted to open the car door and jump. That car ride was one of the worst times in my life. I was just mincemeat. All it took was one car ride and I was a gibbering bloody wreck.

Many controlling men use intimidatory tactics but stop short of violence. When they realise you are determined to separate, this can change. Some men will go to any lengths to prevent their partner from leaving. Tread cautiously. If your partner is threatening violence, always take these threats seriously. Even a man who has never been violent before can erupt into violence when he realises you are intent on leaving. Consider yourself and your children at risk, and act accordingly.

Strategies to ensure your safety before the break-up

- Don't wait until there is a violent attack. Leave as soon as possible.

- Find out the phone number for the local women's refuge. (See 'Community Resources', p. 244.) Contact the refuge for help and advice: that's what they are there for. Keep the number handy at all times.
- Get a friend to stay with you. This may deter your partner from violence while you plan your escape.
- Have an excuse prepared so you can get out of the house if your partner becomes threatening. Drop everything and go if you need to.
- If possible, arrange for neighbours to help in a crisis.
- Make sure your children know what to do in an emergency: who they should phone and where to go for help. Give them the phone numbers they need for the police, neighbours and relatives.
- Keep any important documents, necessary medication and a change of clothes for yourself and the children at a friend's in case you have to leave suddenly.
- Keep a spare set of house and car keys somewhere safe.

What if my partner becomes violent?

It is a good idea to have an escape plan worked out in advance. What will you do if your partner becomes violent? Who will you call for help? If you make a run for it, where will you go and how will you get there? If you feel too overwhelmed to make these decisions alone, ask a refuge worker, counsellor or friend to help you to decide.

Should I contact the police?

The most important consideration is your safety. Each woman needs to decide whether her safety will be increased by involving the police. When you contact the police you are giving your partner the clear message he has overstepped the mark and you will not tolerate his violence. It often has a sobering effect on the man when he realises he's not just dealing with you: involvement with the law means there can be negative consequences for his abusive behaviour. This can be a strong deterrent. On the other hand, there are some men who do not let police involvement stop them. They may even become more aggressive as a result. However, you are generally far better off to seek police protection than to have no protection at all.

The police have a duty to protect you and your children. Family violence now has a higher priority than it once did. If you do need to call the police the following guidelines will be helpful.

Strategies for dealing with the police

- Keep as calm as possible. Tell the police the facts in detail. Show them any injuries you have received and let them know if there are any witnesses, including children.
- Always make sure the police make a report of the incident, even if they do not arrest your partner.
- If you want to, you can ask the police to transport you to a women's refuge or some other safe place.
- Always get the identification number and name of the police personnel involved. Keep a record of the date and time of your call, in case you need to follow it up later.

Other strategies to use if your partner becomes violent

- If you can, leave the house immediately. If you are on foot, seek refuge with a neighbour or go to a public place where there are other people around.
- Get to a phone and contact a women's refuge. They can pick you up and take you to a safe and confidential house. (See also p. 197.)
- If you have left the home to escape violence but feel you have to return, do not go back until your partner has calmed down.
- If possible get a friend or relative to establish your partner's state of mind before returning, and ask him or her to return with you.
- Seek legal advice about obtaining a court order for your protection whether or not you intend to continue living with him. (See p. 237 for further information.)
- If your partner does assault and injure you, always seek

medical treatment. Make sure the doctor knows that the injuries were caused by your partner. Give complete and accurate details about the attack and ask her or him to record these fully. This report may be needed for evidence in future court hearings.

- Alternatively, show any injuries to a friend so she can be a witness if necessary. Get her to take photos of your injuries as evidence.

My partner is leaving me

Sometimes it is the controlling man who makes the decision to leave. For some women this is an answer to a prayer, but for others it is the final blow to their battered self-esteem. They are thrust out of the relationship, shocked and unprepared, robbed of the satisfaction of making a choice and the chance to plan for their own future. In their devastation they are ill-equipped to tackle the multitude of decisions they face.

> Ben just came home one day and announced that he'd written a list of his priorities for life and that me and the kids weren't on it. That was it. I had three small children and I was seven months' pregnant. He told me we could leave after the baby was born. He thought he was being really nice giving me a few months' notice so I could have the baby first. I was totally shattered. I went into counselling because I was so immobilised. That was really helpful. By seeing the counsellor each week I could keep from panicking. At that stage I couldn't even think straight and a lot of what she focused on was just day-to-day survival stuff, like where I was going to live and what I was going to do. I didn't tell the people in my town immediately because I was too embarrassed. That was a big mistake because I was just isolated with my problem. I felt I just had to face it alone. But what I know now is that I would have got support if I had told and that was what I needed.

In time, most women agree that their partner's departure turned out to be a blessing in disguise. Many admit they would not have made the break themselves because they believed themselves responsible for the relationship problems. Others later realise that they were unaware of just how bad things were or how much better their lives could be without their partners. Their only regret was that they lost the opportunity to salvage what was left of their dignity by making the break themselves.

Making the break

Most women agree that the very worst part of the break-up is just before the actual move. Poised on the brink of that life-changing step, our hearts, heads and emotions often pull us in different directions. We may swing back and forth between resignation and panic. As we wait for the right moment to make a move, our fear and anticipation may build almost to fever pitch. Sometimes when the moment of action finally comes, we find a sense of calmness and inner certainty.

> It was weird the day I left. I was suicidal at the time and I'd been diagnosed as a manic depressive. I was a real mess. I went away for a few days and had every intention of going back, but the further away from home I got, the better I felt. That had been happening for quite a while. I'd go out for the afternoon and when I went home I'd get to the end of the street and this horrible, horrible feeling of dread would come over me. This time it was the same, only worse. I decided if going home was going to make me feel that bad, then I wasn't going to be there any more.

Strategies for the break-up

- If you move out, arrange to have someone to help you. This gives you vital moral support.
- Take with you as many of your valuable and treasured possessions as possible or leave them somewhere beforehand. You may not have the opportunity to get them later.
- Take bank books and credit cards and all important

documents with you. Birth and Marriage Certificates, driver's licence, passports, insurance papers, and so on. You will need identification to apply for a benefit.

- Take your children with you if you can. If not, get them as soon as possible. If there is any custody dispute, it is much better if you already have the children with you.
- Take your name off all credit cards and bank accounts immediately, even if you don't think you need to. It pays not to take chances.
- Withdraw half the money from any joint bank account as soon as you can. You may not have the chance later.

Acknowledge the courage it took to break free

Most of us finally leave when we are at our lowest ebb. It takes remarkable courage to choose to take that step at a time when we may just be holding on to life.

> That very first night when I went to bed I felt really strange. Sort of shellshocked. I couldn't believe I'd done it. I didn't know what I felt. All I knew was, if I hadn't got him out, I wouldn't have survived. I knew I had to hold onto that, so I took out a piece of paper and wrote on it. 'Today I have taken a massive step forward, away from death and towards life. Thank God for my will to live. I can make it, and I will.' After that, it was like I felt the tiniest flicker inside me, a flash of a memory of how I used to be, and suddenly I thought, 'My old spark is going to come back. I'm going to be all right.' It was a moment of real relief and thankfulness.

Most of us take our courage for granted or minimise it by saying we had no choice but to leave. Instead of doing this, we need to acknowledge our strength in meeting one of the biggest challenges we may ever face. We may have a long way to go on our journey, but we should never forget the sheer courage it took to take that one crucial step that changed our lives.

Chapter Twelve

Stepping Into a New Beginning

Feel the earth beneath your feet. Feel the air on your face

– from *Notes From The Song of Life*, Tolbert McCarroll

Our first few steps into freedom are likely to be faltering. Many of us begin the journey into our new life from a place of inner devastation.

> Soon after he left, I woke up one morning and it was like I was in this terrible desert. There was nothing familiar. No landmarks. Not even a piece of tussock anywhere to tell me where I was or where to go next.

It takes time to find our way through that desert. Faith is the light that guides us, that belief that we are entitled to something better. We may be unsure what it is and have no idea where to find it, but if we keep taking small steps our oasis will eventually appear.

This chapter will guide you through some of the challenges you are likely to encounter on your journey into freedom.

The early days

> Even though it was my choice to go, I left through blinding tears. I still remember that first night. I was absolutely exhausted. About three in the morning I was on my own and this horrific panic overtook me, and I suddenly thought, 'What have I done? Here I am out in the big wide world, all alone with two kids. Why have I done this? How can I cope on my own?' It was real fear.

Then I thought, 'Hang on. I've just got to take this one
step at a time. I need to get myself off to bed.' The next
morning when I woke up, I thought, 'This is a new day,
a new beginning. I've got to take this very slowly.'

After the initial wrench of the break-up, many of us
experienced a euphoric sense of relief. We'd made it! We were
free! This euphoria carried us through the first days or weeks,
but then it gave way to a time of numbness. We seemed to
be operating on automatic pilot. We were going through the
motions of living, but life didn't quite seem real.

Then gradually the feelings we had been repressing for
so long began to bubble up. Our sorrow, regrets, doubts,
panic, rage and sadness surfaced. Although we were frightened by the intensity of these feelings, we had no option but
to ride them out. Most of us didn't realise it at the time, but
this was an important part of our healing. In allowing and
expressing our feelings, we were reclaiming our real selves.
(See 'Allow yourself to grieve', p. 204.)

Your reaction to breaking up may be similar to this or it
may be quite different. However you experience your
separation is the right way for you. The most important thing
to remember is that you must take good care of yourself
during this time. Make your survival and healing your highest
priority, and remind yourself constantly that you are the most
important person in your life.

You will probably have dozens of practical problems to
overcome: breaking the news to children and relatives,
shifting house, applying for a benefit and obtaining legal
advice. In the midst of all of this, don't forget to take time
out for yourself. When you are becoming overwhelmed,
remember to stop and ask yourself: 'How am I feeling and
what do I need?' Make a point of giving yourself extra care
as often as you can. Do positive things that you know give
you comfort and help you to release your feelings. One of
the women I interviewed spent hours in the bath painting
her fingernails. Another often went running, letting the tears
pour down her face as she ran. Another would pretend her
husband was right there in the room with her, and would

tell him just what she thought of him. Do whatever you need to do. However, beware of the dangers of using alcohol or drugs in an attempt to numb the pain. Over-indulgence in these escapes can create other problems for you to deal with. If you feel you are developing a problem in either of these areas, see 'If you have a problem with alcohol or drugs', pp. 101.)

The secret of making it through the bad times is to stay focused on the here and now. Looking back can swamp you with memories; looking forward can engulf you with fear. But if you stay right where you are, and concentrate on giving yourself what you need in that moment, you will be all right. When you are feeling panicky, try taking a slow, deep breath and saying to yourself, 'Right now, in this moment, I am safe.'

Reach out for all the support, love and encouragement you can get. This is not the time to go it alone. Don't be too independent to allow your family and friends to give you help. No doubt the time will come when they will need your help and you will be able to return the favour.

There are bound to be some challenging moments in the days ahead. Accepting these times as a natural part of the separation process will help you to get through them. It really is true that when one door closes another one opens. The void in your life that your partner leaves will soon be filled with new people and activities that will be far more life-enhancing.

Exercise: Recording the bad memories

Because our memories play tricks on us, and the same denial that kept us hanging in there for so long still operates at times, it is important to record what has happened.

As soon as possible after the break-up, write yourself two lists:

1. The things my partner did that hurt me are . . .
2. The ways this affected me were . . . (include: your symptoms of distress, the ways you have changed, lost opportunities, how you felt, the impact on other relationships, the deterioration in your health, and so on).

These lists need to be kept and added to as you become clearer about some of the things that you have experienced.

When the going gets tough and you start to feel that life with your partner wasn't so bad after all, re-read these lists to remind you of what you have been through and why you made the break for freedom.

Dealing with your ex-partner

Some of us are lucky enough to be able to break ties completely with the man who abused us. However great a wrench, it gives us complete freedom to rebuild our lives. For other women the break is not so easy. When children are involved, we are forced to maintain ties with our ex-partner. This contact may give our ex-partner further opportunities to undermine and abuse us; contact can be dominated by his demands, lack of co-operation and respect, game-playing and broken promises.

Even after the separation, trying to stay strong enough to stand up for our rights and set limits with our partner can be an on-going challenge.

Strategies for dealing with your ex-partner

- Prepare yourself emotionally and mentally before contact with your ex-partner. Remember you are in charge of your own life and he has no right to try to control you.
- When you see your ex-partner, consider having someone with you for moral support.
- Set limits about your ex-partner's behaviour. Refuse to let him put you down. Write a list of what you will not tolerate. Terminate the encounter if he will not respect your rights.
- Remain clear about the purpose of your contact. If he wishes to raise issues outside of that, make another appointment so you can prepare yourself.
- If you find yourself drawn back by his charm or promises, re-read your 'bad memories' lists.
- Make a note of all arrangements and agreements, so your partner can't play 'twist the truth' and denial games.

It may take time before we're confident enough to set clear limits on our partner's behaviour but, when we do, it is a personal victory.

> Dave used to just arrive at my place unannounced and walk in. I'd get home from work and he'd be standing in my kitchen cooking. I found this an invasion of my privacy, but I was too scared to say anything. One night I arrived home full of champagne and I thought, 'No, I've had enough, I can't stand him doing this any more.' I walked in and screamed at him at the top of my voice, which I never usually did, told him in very colourful language to get out. Without a word, he dropped what he was doing, scuttled out of the house and drove off in his car. He never did that again.

Staying safe after the break-up

If your partner has been violent in the past, you are likely to find the first weeks out of the relationship fraught with anxiety. Your safety may have depended on knowing where your partner was and what mood he was in; now, without that knowledge, you may feel even more vulnerable and afraid. Get as much support for yourself as possible during this time. Fear of your partner is not a good reason for being tempted to return to him.

If you are concerned about your safety, consider staying in a women's refuge, at least initially. Its address is confidential, and the refuge can arrange to place you in a different area if necessary. (See 'The role of Women's Aid', p. 183.)

Strategies to increase your safety after the break-up

- Take any threats seriously and report them to the police.
- Seek legal advice and arrange to have a court order taken out against your partner. That will ban him from having any contact with you. If your partner breaks this order, he can be arrested. (See p. 237 for details about obtaining a court order.)

- After you have obtained the court order, notify the police *every time* your partner attempts to make contact with you. If you are consistent about this, your partner will soon realise you mean business.
- If you are frightened of your partner but don't obtain a court order, at the very least refuse to be alone with him. For necessary contact go through a third person, preferably a lawyer.
- If you need to return home at a later date to collect your belongings, ask the police to accompany you.
- If you stay in the house, change all locks. If possible, arrange for the neighbours to keep a watch over you, and phone the police if necessary.
- Consider getting an unlisted telephone number.

Discovering who you are now

One of the best parts of beginning a new life is getting to know ourselves again. Having denied our own truth, and had our opinions squashed and our choices blocked for so long, we are free to be ourselves. But, at first, many of us don't know how to begin.

> When I first came out of the marriage I didn't really have a clue who I was or what I liked, so it was really important for me to find role models. Now that I had choices, I needed to know what clothes I liked and how I'd like to decorate a home. I started cutting pictures of the things I liked out of magazines and putting them into a scrapbook. I also cut out pictures of women who I admired in some way, and was amazed at the different ones I chose. It was not that I was putting these women up on a pedestal. I just needed to realise that there were women out there doing things, that they were safe doing them, and I might want to do some of those things myself one day. Just to realise that there were possibilities for my future was so important.

The gift of creativity

Our creativity is an expression of who we really are, so reclaiming it is an important part of our healing. (See 'Loss of creativity', p. 50.) Our creativity nurtures us emotionally, mentally, physically and spiritually, and though it may have been crushed in the relationship, it always remains a part of us. Some women find that they have many remarkable gifts which have been lying dormant, just waiting to be discovered.

> Since I've been on my own I've found I have talents that I didn't even know I had. This discovery has been the most exciting thing that's ever happened to me. Only in the last few years I have realised I can sing. I've got an amazing voice, not just an ordinary voice. I think what shocked me was that I never even knew I had it. It was suppressed and hidden because of the situation I was in. I'm angry to think I've missed out on years when I could have sung and definitely made money out of it. But still, I have it for myself now. I've also discovered I can paint and write really well, and I had no idea about that either. Being able to pursue these talents is just so exciting. It's like I've got a second chance at life.

Exercise: Reclaiming your creativity

Spend some time exploring these questions in your journal.
- Do you have any interests or talents that you have put on hold, even since childhood?
- Before the relationship began, what activities gave you pleasure?
- How can you make these things part of your life now?
- What interests and pleasures did you want to pursue while you were in the relationship, but were unable to?
- How can you bring these into being now?
- What gives you joy and makes you feel alive?
- How can you bring more of these things into your life now?

Wanting to go back

> I resisted the urge to see him for several months because I still loved him and I didn't trust myself. I used my memories and anger as a defence, but eventually they began to fade. One night I suddenly had this over-

whelming desire to see Paul, to hear his voice and feel his arms around me. I just wanted him so much that nothing else mattered. I didn't care any more. I forgot all the rotten times, his coldness and cruelty. Everything! Thank God I rang a friend before doing it, and she talked some sense into me. If I'd given in, I'd have lost everything I'd gained and been right back where I started.

In the early days building a new life can be lonely, exhausting and distressing. There are moments when most of us long to give up and return to the familiarity of our old life. As the memories of the bad times fade, the rosy memories of the happier times can undermine our resolve. Going back to our partner can seem like a seductively simple solution to the problems that surround us. If you get the urge to go back, try asking yourself:

- Why do I want to go back?
- What has triggered those feelings?
- If I see my partner now, what am I hoping the outcome will be?
- If I go back to him, how do I honestly see the future?

We can tell ourselves that we would be better off with our abusive partner, but the chances are we won't be. Staying confined in a destructive relationship can be a life sentence in which the pain only gets worse.

It is during the first months, when we are just beginning to rebuild our lives, that we are most at risk of wanting to go back to our ex-partner. We need to anticipate these moments and have strategies in place to help us overcome them.

Strategies for resisting going back

- Arrange ahead of time to phone a friend when the urge to go back strikes. Phone her before taking any action. Have her remind you of all the reasons you left.
- Talk through the feelings that are making you want to go back. When these feelings are acknowledged openly, they lose much of their power. If you have no one to share your feelings with, try expressing them in your journal.

- Remind yourself about how your partner's abuse affected you by re-reading the 'bad memories' lists you wrote soon after leaving (see p. 195). Get back into your anger about his mistreatment.
- Focus on the here and now, not the future. Recognise that this is a bad moment that will pass. Do something for yourself right now that will make you feel better.
- Transfer your distress into positive action. One woman gradually redecorated her whole house in this way.

If, having followed these strategies, you still feel you want to go back, it can be a good idea to take your time. Rather than returning on impulse, try giving yourself a week to think it over before putting the wheels of change in motion. During that week, review again what your life was really like with your partner, and talk through your options, fears and concerns with a counsellor or supportive friend.

Resisting sexual attraction

If good sex has been a feature of the relationship, it can be difficult to break that bond. But continuing a sexual relationship with our ex-partner only prolongs the agony of the break-up. It also makes us vulnerable to going back when it is not in our best interests to do so. It is better to avoid the risk. A clean break is painful, but leaves us free to grieve for our losses and rebuild our separate life.

> It took me a long time to pull away physically. Brett had the capacity to make me melt. He'd ring me up and be so charming and caring. Then he'd come and see me, and hold me so securely in his arms. It felt so good. It'd start out as a cuddle but I just couldn't resist him – one kiss and I was history. Afterwards it made me feel worse. I was still having all these heart feelings for Brett, but really it was just sex for him.

The decision to try again

> I had to give it one more try before the realisation finally sank in that it was not going to work. I went back

thinking maybe it will be better because I've learned about myself. But Jeff hadn't changed, and because of what I'd learned I now had to bend myself a little harder to fit the circumstances.

Although many women manage to make a clean break, some of us make at least one attempt at reconciliation. Our hope may have been rekindled by our partner's reassurances, or we may have become disillusioned in our attempts to go it alone. When we try again, there is often a honeymoon period. However, unless our partner is committed to working at change, we are soon likely to find ourselves treading the same painful path that led to break-up.

For some women, a first break gives them a taste of freedom that empowers them to leave again if they need to. For others who did not give themselves time to get on their feet alone, the memory of that difficult separation can become a barrier to any future break-up. If you decide to go back, be very clear about why you are making that decision, and how long you will give your partner to make positive changes before making a final separation. How will you know if the time comes to leave again? What will your limit be? Without answers to these important questions it is possible to waste many precious years of our lives going down the same dead-end track, as many of us can testify.

Becoming free

Although we have physically separated from our partner, we may still feel connected to him on many other levels. That sense of connection can drain our energy and prevent us from feeling completely free. The following visualisation will help you to disconnect from your partner and reclaim the energy you gave him when you were in the relationship. (See also 'Completing with your ex-partner', p. 208.)

Visualisation Exercise: Breaking the ties

Close your eyes, breathe deeply and freely, and allow yourself to relax. Imagine you're standing alone on a long beach. You are surrounded by an invisible shield of protection that cannot be penetrated. You feel completely safe, protected and supported by the power of nature that surrounds you. Take some time to absorb this strength.

Imagine you see your partner in the distance. Notice how you feel. Remember you are completely safe. Invite your partner to come toward you and tell him to stop at a distance that you feel comfortable with. You notice that you are connected to him by several silver cords. These cords run from your sexual, emotional, heart, vocal, intellectual and spiritual centres to his. The thickness of each cord corresponds to the strength of the connection between you at that level. Notice the different strengths of those connections.

When you are ready, imagine yourself reaching out and gently disconnecting these cords from your body, one by one. As you disconnect each cord, imagine that that energy centre in you is filled with healing light and feel the increase in your energy.

As you disconnect the cords, say to your partner, 'I am in my own power now. I choose to separate from you. All of myself that I have given to you, and that you have taken, I reclaim. I set myself free.' When you have finished, express anything else you still need to say to your partner briefly, then say goodbye.

Watch as your partner turns and walks away from you, gradually disappearing into the distance. As he vanishes on the horizon, a bright golden light rises up into the sky from where he disappeared. It stops in front of you and surrounds you with its radiance and says, 'I am all of you that you had lost.' Feel that energy coming back into your body, filling you with strength and wholeness.

Chapter Thirteen

Healing the Wounds

The deeper that sorrow carves into your being, the more joy you can contain

— from *The Prophet*, Kahlil Gibran

Recovery is a journey which may at times be challenging and harrowing, but ultimately it is freeing. In a sense it is about coming home to ourselves.

Sadly, there may be little to be salvaged from the wreckage of the relationship: no respect, honesty, co-operation or friendship. The heartbreak of facing this devastation after perhaps years of effort can make healing a slow and difficult process. In this chapter the women I interviewed join me in sharing the ways we are coming to terms with our sorrow, healing our wounds and emotionally freeing ourselves to lead satisfying lives.

Allow yourself to grieve

Grieving is an important part of the recovery process. Even if we count ourselves lucky for having left our destructive relationship, we have sustained many losses along the way — years of our life, our innocence and trust, our hopes and dreams, our homes, lifestyle and financial security. Our family unit has been broken. We may miss the security and comfort of having a partner there. The companionship, intimacy and fun that were shared during the good moments is over.

We are entitled to grieve not only for all that has ended, but also for what never was and for what might have been. We need to grieve for the happiness we have missed, and the harm that has been done to our self-esteem, health and relationships with others. Grieving is about facing and moving through our sorrow at these losses.

Many of us strongly resist our grief. We feel we have wasted enough of our lives, and want to put the past behind us.

> I was stuck in denial for a long time after the marriage ended. I shoved everything inside me and started a new life that was totally different. I didn't want to think about the past any more. I just wanted to get on with it. I know now that just wasn't feasible. I developed a serious, stress-related illness, and I realised I wouldn't recover unless I faced everything in my life that needed to be faced.

The grief we do not express remains locked within. As well as deadening our positive emotions and darkening our view of the future, it may affect our physical health, cause us to behave self-destructively and prevent us from trusting and loving fully again. The way out of grief is through it. Bitter tears, despair and rage are all part of our healing, and we need to allow ourselves the time and space to express them.

I've heard grief described as a 'jagged journey', and that's certainly the way I've experienced it. Just when I think I am getting over what has happened, a particularly sharp memory plunges me back into the depths again. But I hold onto the knowledge that this jagged journey will not last for ever. I know that every day I move through my grief, I am a day closer to emotional freedom.

Each of us experiences grief in our own unique way. Many women go through a period of depression. This is a normal response to any major change and loss in our lives. Most women also get in touch with the full intensity of the anger they have spent years repressing. This anger is not unhealthy or 'bad', as we have been taught. In fact it can be life-giving.

> I didn't start to feel angry until I realised that what had happened wasn't all my fault. What John did to me was not right. It was awful! I had every right to feel angry at him, because he'd hurt me. It was as simple as that.

When I finally found my anger, I used it to fuel me on.
It was so healthy. I'd just think, 'Who the hell is he to
mess me up for the rest of my life? It's just not worth it.
I'm going to get over this.' My anger just freed me. I
knew I didn't have to act on my anger or to lash out
with it. I just allowed myself to feel it and let it go when
I was ready. Gradually as I came to terms with things, it
just faded away.

Share your story

During our times of grief and healing, we need to be gentle
with ourselves and seek the support we need. In my
experience there is nothing as healing as trusting another
person with my story and feeling that person has really heard
and accepted what I'm saying. That person's gift of acceptance
breaks through my self-doubt and confusion, and helps me
to heal my deep wounds. As I share my story I am finding
out about myself in a way that it is not possible to do in
isolation.

Friends are a wonderful source of comfort. People in
support groups who have shared experiences and are on a
similar journey also provide a very special kind of caring.

I went to a support group and got a lot of my feelings
out there. I didn't really start to grieve before that. I was
so into being strong for my kids. I just wanted them to
be happy, so I went on pretending I was happy, but really
I was just knotted up inside. In the group I felt safe
enough to stop being so strong and to give up my
control. I really opened up. I realised that there was real
anger in me. I was always a kind and loving, happy-go-
lucky person. I never realised I'd suppressed so much
anger. There were so many things that other people said
in that group that had happened to me too. That was a
big surprise, and it made me feel a lot better about
myself. Really we supported each other and we'd ring
each other and talk and talk. It really made a huge
difference in my life.

In most communities there are many groups offering

opportunities for support and personal growth. These include support groups for the newly separated, or for women recovering from abusive relationships; self-assertion training groups; women's spirituality groups, and confidence-building groups. All have something to offer to our healing.

Being part of a group gives us the opportunity to share what we have learned. Reaching out to other people who are hurting is part of our healing. When we reach out with compassion from the depth of our own experience, we are offering an invaluable gift.

Write yourself free

Your journal can be a wonderful means of self expression during your time of healing.

> Writing down my feelings every day helped me such a lot. It lifted me! No matter how painful my feelings were, I learned not to push them away. I'd write about them until they didn't hurt any more. And as I wrote I'd visualise those words coming from deep inside me and tell myself that once they were out on the paper they weren't inside me to hurt any more. From there I could choose what I did with them. Sometimes I'd put my writing aside until later and then re-read it to see if I could work out what had triggered those feelings. Other times I'd burn the paper and throw the ashes into the wind, and focus on letting go.

Exercise: Writing from your heart

Write about your journey through your relationship. What has it meant to you emotionally, physically and spiritually? Express your grief about your losses. Write about your wounds and how you're going to heal them. What do you need to help you heal? Which of your strengths will you draw on to sustain you? Honour in your writing how far you have come and all you have achieved. Explore your hopes for the future. Let your writing guide you through your pain to a place of renewed hope.

If possible, share your writing with a trustworthy friend or your support group. Speaking our truth out loud helps to free us from pain.

Completing with your ex-partner

Even after we are physically separated from our ex-partner, it is possible for him to dominate our thoughts, feelings and behaviour for a long time.

> For the first two years I definitely wasn't free of Jim. It was like I was still carrying him around in my head. I could still hear him criticising me, and that stopped me from doing a lot of things. I thought about the relationship constantly. I'd have these running conversations in my head where I'd be asking Jim why he treated me like that, and trying to make him understand how he'd hurt me. Then I realised that while I was doing this, I was wasting even more of my time. Instead of making a new life for myself, I was stuck in the past. By constantly thinking about him, I was giving him ongoing power over me which he didn't even have.

When we separate we need to reclaim not only our physical space but also our mind space. One of the biggest difficulties is that we have often left so many things unsaid.

> I'm still angry and hurt because there are a million things that I desperately need to say to Peter which I'll never have the chance to say. For once I'd like to state my version of what happened, and let him know how I felt during those awful times. I really wish I'd been able to stand up to him at the time, but I didn't dare. Now it's too late, and that really gets to me. I've got all this stuff going around in my head and no way of dealing with it.

Two possible ways of resolving your feelings are to write to your ex-partner or to confront him face to face.

Exercise: Write to your ex-partner

Writing your ex-partner a letter, or series of letters, which express exactly how you feel can be a powerful way of soothing inner turmoil and releasing the past. If you write these letters for yourself only, and not for sending to your ex-partner, you can express your deepest feelings openly, without concern for how he may react. Your letter could include:

- the memories that are still troubling you;
- the things you were unable to say at the time;
- the ways your ex-partner has affected your life.

Because writing at this depth can bring up intense feelings, it is a good idea to set aside an uninterrupted time to write in privacy. When you have completed your letter, sharing it with a friend, counsellor or support group can help to make you feel more complete. You may then choose to destroy the letter while focusing on letting go of the past. You may even want to modify your letter and send it to your ex-partner.

Confronting your ex-partner

Confronting your ex-partner face to face while staying in your own power can be an important step in recovery. Before directly confronting him, you need to be sure that you feel strong enough to cope with his reactions. If safety is an issue, any confrontation will need to be done in the presence of others, perhaps in your counsellor's office. It is important not to have any expectations that your ex-partner will behave in a caring way. He probably won't, but if you are doing this for your own empowerment that need not matter.

> It had been eighteen months since we split up and there'd been no contact. That was good in a way, but it also left me feeling up in the air. Eventually I figured out I needed to face Wayne. Really I needed to know that he no longer had the power to hurt me. I was shaking in my shoes all the way to his place, but I just kept affirming that I had the power to deal with whatever happened, and that helped me to feel stronger. He hadn't changed, but the most wonderful thing was, I had! He used all his usual tactics to bully me and shut me up. It was nerve-wracking and hurtful to sit through

it, and at first I started to panic. Then I realised I was okay. It was like he was throwing all this crap and none of it was touching me. It just didn't matter any more. I managed to say the couple of things I needed to say before leaving when I was ready, not when he ordered me out. Afterwards I was absolutely elated. I'd stood my ground. He didn't have the power to hurt me any more and he knew it. I was free.

Strategies for confronting

- *Plan ahead of time.* Where and when will you confront him? What are you hoping to achieve? What do you need to say?

- *Rehearse what you will say.* Be clear about the points you want to make. It is best to keep the message fairly brief and direct.

- *Get support for yourself.* Plan and practise with a friend or counsellor, and talk through your feelings before and after the confrontation. Consider taking a support person with you.

- *Prepare for the worst.* It is highly likely that your ex-partner will try all his usual tactics on you. He may deny, accuse, blame or become self-righteous or self-pitying. You will need to be prepared to stand your ground and not be drawn in by these tactics.

Completing the grief process

As we have seen, grieving the loss of a relationship is an important part of the rebuilding process. We will always remember what has happened, but one of our goals can be that we reach a stage where those memories no longer have the power to hurt us in the same way. Then the past cannot poison the future.

Counselling or courses specially designed to help people resolve their grief after separation or the death of a partner provide a gentle yet powerful means of closing the door on a relationship. The support and safety provided allows participants to explore and express their feelings, re-evaluate their lives and move into the future with renewed hope. (See 'Community Resources', p. 244, for details.)

> I knew I needed to do something for myself to help me get over Tim, so I decided to do a 'Beginning Experience' [a weekend programme run by the Catholic Church] weekend. I was terribly scared going on my own, but it was an amazing weekend. I realised I'd been so busy getting on with things that I'd just locked my feelings away inside. Really they needed to be resolved. The weekend helped me to face my pain and heal it. It also helped me to face facts and accept things as they are. There was a lot of support and I had my tears, but afterwards I felt ready to put it behind me and go on with my life in a positive way. I felt a real inner peace, totally cleansed. It was really wonderful.

The possibility of forgiveness

To complete our healing, the only person whom it is vital to forgive is ourselves. Instead of blaming ourselves for trying too hard for too long, being too trusting, putting our partner's well-being ahead of our own, or being unable to protect ourselves fully, we need to forgive ourselves. We may also need to forgive ourselves for the destructive ways we have reacted toward others because of our pain, and the ways we have neglected, abused or failed to protect our children.

Carrying the burden of guilt for the mistakes we have made will not erase yesterday's actions. It will prevent us from coming to terms with the past and moving on. If we have genuinely hurt another person through our actions, then honestly acknowledging this to the person concerned, and offering an apology, can help. After that, we need to accept we have done all we can and let it go.

Deciding whether to forgive the man who has hurt and betrayed us is an individual choice. It is possible to recover from the abuse we have suffered without forgiving our ex-partner. Finding some kind of resolution within ourselves is the important thing. If we decide to forgive him, the only person we should do it for is ourself. We do not *owe* our partner forgiveness. We certainly do not need to forgive him so he can feel better. Forgiving does not change the fact of his abuse.

Forgiveness needs to come after we have had time to express our grief fully over what has happened. Some people may encourage us to forgive quickly because they are uncomfortable with our grief, especially our expression of anger. Quick forgiveness is not a shortcut to feeling better. Forgiving too early robs us of the chance to work through our feelings. When we are denied the opportunity to express our anger, we may sink into depression instead.

Forgiveness often takes place gradually, after we have expressed and moved through all the stages of grief. Occasionally forgiveness can happen spontaneously, once the decision has been made.

> It was about a year after the break-up, and I was lying on the beach listening to a woman on the radio talking about forgiveness. Apparently, to forgive I didn't have to go to the person but just needed to speak it and mean it. Everything had been festering away inside me and I'd got to the stage where I couldn't cope with it any more. I thought, 'If it gives me freedom from this awful pain, then it's worth it.' Inside my head I said, 'I forgive you for all the hurt you caused me and for not loving me the way I needed you to love me.' All the aching stopped and it was such a relief. I thought, 'Yes, I've let go, and I don't have to put any more energy into Grant's life. It is all for me. I'm not tied to him any more.' I felt like I'd set myself free.

Healing past wounds

If we have been wounded by verbal, emotional, physical or sexual abuse as children, we are vulnerable to abuse again as adults. (See 'Childhood abuse', p. 65.) Until we have healed those early wounds, we will never really be free to live fully. The better we know and understand our story, the less likelihood there is of us repeating our early childhood patterns in our adult life.

There are many ways we can begin to heal our childhood wounds. We can allow ourselves to remember those painful memories of abuse and re-experience the emotions that have been buried with them. We can explore these memories and emotions with a therapist, share them in a support group and write about them in our journal. We can also move out of numb denial and reclaim our anger about that abuse, and direct that anger at our original abuser instead of ourself. We can grieve for the loss of our childhood innocence and the betrayal of our trust; for the feelings of confusion, shame and guilt we have carried through our lives. We can grieve for the battering our self-esteem took and the way that continues to affect us today; for the on-going pain we experience and the years spent grimly coping. We can spend time rediscovering and getting to know our bruised and frightened inner child. We can learn to comfort, nurture and encourage her, just as we would any child who was hurting.

Healing deep wounds takes time. Being without a partner can give us a unique opportunity to gain this time.

> After the break-up I took a hard look at my life and I could see that the ways I had been abused in my relationship were very similar to the ways my father had abused me as a child. I knew if I didn't deal with that first abuse I might get involved with another abusive man and go down that path again. That was my greatest fear, so I made a decision I wouldn't have another relationship for at least a year, and during that time I'd do my best to come to terms with my back-ground, and to build a much stronger sense of self. In the meantime, I wrote myself a list of the things I was not willing to

tolerate in an intimate relationship ever again, so I'd find it much harder to repeat those same patterns again. I decided then and there that if any man I was involved with tried to control me again, that was it. I felt a lot stronger after that, just knowing I had some clear limits that no one was going to step over. That gave me the space to begin to really work on myself.

In healing our past we are setting ourselves free to lead satisfying lives. We are completing the journey home to our self.

Creating a brighter future

In the early stages of separation, an unknown future can be frightening to contemplate. But this fear gradually begins to change as we heal.

For a long time when I tried to look ahead I'd think, 'What's the point? There's no future,' and I'd just burst into tears. It seemed that every dream I'd had had gone wrong or been taken away from me. Now I'm slowly inching my way forward. My plans may only go one week ahead, but at least I do believe there is a future, and I'm allowing myself to have dreams again – just very little dreams.

Today's dreams are tomorrow's reality. One of the most positive steps any of us can take towards creating a brighter future is to set goals. Setting goals is not about struggling and striving; it is about identifying some of the infinite possibilities for our future. Goal-setting rekindles our hope, creates opportunities and opens new doors. It is an act of power. As we open our minds and hearts to new possibilities, we are saying 'yes' to life.

In setting goals it is not necessary to know exactly how we will achieve them. It is amazing how, when a definite decision to go in a particular direction has been made, everything begins to fall into place – and often in ways we would never have anticipated.

As part of my recovery, I began to write myself a list of the things I'd like to do. One of the things I wanted was to visit my sister in Sydney. Here I was with no money, debts and terrible trauma all around me, yet three months after writing this on my list I ended up in Sydney. And I hadn't even told anyone I had it on my list.

Exercise: Dare to dream

Create a list of the things you would like to do. Make it as varied and as fanciful as you like. Express your secret passions. Try beginning your list: 'If anything were possible I'd like to . . .'

Don't limit yourself by wondering how you could achieve your dreams. Just allow yourself to have them. You will probably be surprised by how many of these dreams become reality over time, once you have identified them. The list can be expanded as you conceive new ideas.

Setting specific goals

Ideally we should write down the goals we set for ourselves. This takes them out of the realm of vague wishes, and captures them in a tangible form. Goals need to be specific and measurable so that we know when we have reached them. Short-term goals should be highly achievable, as success is a wonderful confidence-booster that spurs us on to greater things. When we set long-term goals we can open our imagination to bolder possibilities. It is okay to be bold when we set long-term goals, because they can be changed or discarded at any time.

Set a feasible time frame for reaching your goals. If you do not achieve your goals, it may be that the time frame was unrealistic and needs to be changed, that the goal was set too high and needs to be broken into smaller goals, or that the goal is no longer important to you. Never give yourself a hard time if you do not meet your goals. The purpose of having goals is to enhance your life by opening up new opportunities, not to create feelings of stress and failure.

Strategies for goal-setting

- *Create a goal-setting book for yourself.* You can then look back over your goals in the future and remind yourself how far you've come.
- *Make goal-setting a special time.* Put on some inspirational music, light a candle, burn some incense. Focus within and ask for guidance.
- *Try setting goals for the different areas of your life*: home, relationships, education, personal growth, employment, finances and leisure-time activities.
- *Write your goals as short, specific statements set in the present tense.* This makes them seem more immediate and obtainable. Use these statements as affirmations which help condition your mind to expect success.
- *Break your goals down into manageable steps.* When taking those steps, focus on the desired result rather than the small details of how you will get there. Faith moves mountains!
- *Picture your goals often, as if you have already achieved them.* A clear vision of where we want to go creates a powerful blueprint.
- *Revise and rewrite your goals regularly.* Modify those that have changed and discard those that are no longer valid.
- *Don't forget to congratulate yourself on the goals you have achieved!*

Exercise: Exploring the possibilities

Before setting goals, explore your hopes for the future using the following questions as a guide.
- What are the most important priorities for my future?
- What possibilities fill me with excitement? What would enrich my life?
- How would I like to be living one year from now, five years from now, ten years from now?
- What would I like to achieve personally within these time frames?

When we dare to define what we want for our future, we are

opening the door to big and powerful changes in our lives. From the self-knowledge that these written reflections provide, you can move on to create the bright future you are entitled to. Sometimes we are so busy pushing ahead to the next challenge that we forget to stop and marvel at how far we have come. Try keeping an on-going list to remind you of all you have achieved since leaving the relationship.

The ways women healed their wounds

It is significant that the final stage of this book is being written while I'm on holiday with a group of longstanding, treasured women friends. As we have talked, laughed, walked beside the ocean and swum, I have rediscovered my joy at being alive. I didn't think I would ever feel like my 'old' self again. I realise now that some of my grief has been for that part of me I thought had been crushed for ever. I am so grateful to discover I am still capable of feeling carefree and excited about the future.

Each woman has her own unique way of healing her deep wounding. Writing this book has been my greatest healing. Hearing the stories of other women's journeys has given me a deeper understanding of my own experience. In the process of writing I have been constantly reminded how much we gain by sharing our stories with one another.

The women I interviewed offered many insights into the special, life-giving ways they healed. Their determination to recover and rebuild often provided the impetus for exciting new endeavours. As these women testify, there certainly is life after the abusive man.

Gradually I've developed wonderful new friendships. Many of these people I met at a support group for women on their own; others I have met through becoming involved at my kids' school and playing badminton once a week. I never had many friends when I was married, so I really appreciate that now. Really these friendships are far closer than any I've ever had before.

The only way I ended up making any sense out of my life was by reading. I'd go to the library and get a pile of books out on self-help, women's studies or human development, and I found out I fell into all these boxes. I'd read something in a book and I'd think, 'That's me!' or, 'Far out, someone else has had that exact same thing happen to them.' And it was only by doing that that I realised that my experience was similar to perhaps millions of other women's. Those books validated the way I felt, and that was great.

To find out who I really was I had to disentangle myself from all the emotional garbage that had gone on in my life. So I moved right away from everyone. It was a bit scary at first, but then I realised this was what I really wanted and needed, and it was great. Once I got away, that time was the best in my life. I just seemed to go from strength to strength. I really fell in love with myself. I lost lots of weight, got really fit and even competed in triathlons. I discovered a whole new side of me I didn't even know I had. It was just neat. I'd never felt like that before in my life.

Although it took me quite a while to get my confidence back, getting back to work was really important. I was back in the real world. It was then I realised, by being with others, that there was nothing wrong with me.

I decided to join a tramping club because I didn't want to become isolated, and this seemed a good way to get out to meet new people and get some fresh air and exercise. It's been great! I've made new friends and even had a few weekends away. It is marvellous getting out to enjoy the scenery.

I've set up a support group for women in our community, and this has helped me realise that good things do happen. I'm not stupid. I can actually get things organised and off the ground. It's so exciting to see the women suddenly grow and reach out to support one another. I draw from my own experience a lot, and the other women know where I'm coming from and that

I'm open to share where I've been and what the path was like. It feels great to use my experiences to help others.

My faith has helped tremendously to give me that sense of purpose. My spirituality has developed slowly since my partner left. I listen to my inner voice more now, and my intuition tells me a lot of things. I really believe in the power of positive thinking and have been able to create a good life for us all that way. And for the first time ever, I'm totally in awe of nature. This autumn has been just magic to me. It feels as if everything's just been washed clean and I'm seeing it all in a different light.

Something that helped to empower me was doing a self-defence course. It was a great boost to my self-esteem and confidence. It made me see that I don't have to sit back and take what's dished out. I have the right to be treated with dignity and respect. It opened my mind and brought my fear of attack into perspective. Instead of feeling like a 'weak female', I now have the awareness to deal with a bad situation well.

I decided I was going to do something that was important to me. I've always wanted to dance, so I've joined 'Ceroc', which is a mixture of rock and roll and ballroom dancing. I love it! It's fun and it's fast. I'm meeting people and having a ball. It's really good, because I was so weighed down that I didn't know any more that life could be fun.

The most life-giving and healing thing for me, after what I went through, has been to discover and play with my inner child. What I needed was just lightness and fun. Being with my family, seeing the world through children's eyes and laughing at silly things – I really love that.

It's been so important to learn to laugh. Sometimes I sit down with friends and talk about the past and we'll see the absolutely ridiculous side of it, and we just laugh and laugh. It's actually very therapeutic.

I went out with other men and found out I wasn't a horrible, repulsive, boring person, and that was an important discovery. Other men treated me like an intelligent, attractive human being. And, much to my delight, I found I could have really good sex without being in love with the person. That had never occurred to me before.

I had a wonderful sexual relationship and that was a very important part of my healing. It was the most mind-blowing experience. It was so different. I learned about me as a woman. To be what I wanted to be, and to feel comfortable and safe about doing what I wanted to do. Before that, I had real hang-ups. I thought there was something wrong with me because I didn't want my husband. I felt unattractive and undesirable, because the message he was giving me was that I was wrong. Now I know that part of my life can be good, happy and fantastic.

It was such an exciting moment when I realised that it was up to me where I went from here. I could make my life the way I wanted it to be. I had a choice! I could continue to carry what had happened around with me and let it tarnish the rest of my life, or I could look to my own future. With a new life, anything's possible. Although it's scary not knowing what it's going to bring, it's also incredibly exciting. It's all up to me! Like the song says, it's 'take your passion, and make it happen', and that's what I'm going to do. There's a whole world out there, and I owe it to myself to make the most of it.

Chapter Fourteen

Pearls of Wisdom

The comments in this chapter come from women who have lived through the misery and despair of an abusive relationship and yet have emerged stronger, wiser and determined to move on to brighter and better things. I asked each woman I interviewed what she'd like to pass on to others who are living in destructive relationships. These loving and wise words are their gifts to you.

I'd really like other women to know there are people who care about them. I really wish I could give all those women my phone number. When I was at my worst I thought I was so worthless that nobody would be interested in what I had to say. I was wrong. People do care. Find someone you can really trust to talk to, and get their support.

I'd like to encourage other women to put themselves first, to do whatever they need to do to take care of themselves so they can be strong. Everything else comes second. All through the abuse I felt like there was a child inside me that kept hoping that someone was going to help her. It was so important when I gave up trying to get anyone else to help me and started to do it for myself.

Every woman is an independent, intelligent being in her own right. Nobody has the right to hurt others, either physically or emotionally, or to walk over them for their own gratification. We all need to remember that. We all have the right to a decent life.

I believe it is really important for us to learn to stand up for ourselves and put ourselves first. We have been taught to be caring and compassionate, and even though these are good qualities, they can leave us so defenceless with a controlling man. We really need to learn to be more aware of when someone is a destructive influence in our lives, and be prepared to stop them hurting us. It's okay to give, but remember not to give your whole self away. Save something for yourself!

Even though you might not realise it or feel it at the moment, you are very special and you need to do everything to take care of yourself and to get the help you need. Then you will come to believe in yourself again.

I feel the most important thing is not to give up your friends. Although my partner did his best to break up my friendships, that circle was not broken. My friends were still there waiting for me, and I've had incredible support from them.

Don't believe it if your partner says you are fat or stupid. Give yourself some sort of affirmation. I took on everything that was said, because if someone loved me how could they be wrong? I mean, they wouldn't deliberately hurt me, would they? It took me a long time to realise that the people you love can deliberately hurt you.

Do your best to keep the balance in your life between the relationship, family, friendships, work, recreation and time alone. All these things are important. Do everything you can to build your self-esteem. Put energy into yourself; try to keep your self-confidence intact; hang onto your own beliefs, your calm and your spirituality.

Read books that nourish your sense of self and strength. Gather the things around you that inspire you and continually reflect on them, so that you have something to work towards that is uplifting.

Don't blame yourself for your situation. For years I thought it was all me. I was to blame, because I was one of those 'women who loved too much' and I had come from an alcoholic family. I refuse to take that on now. Maybe I did try harder than I should have, but my partner was the one who took advantage of the love

I gave in good faith. No way am I going to waste any more precious time blaming myself. That's a real trap we fall into as women, and it can be so destructive.

I remember how difficult it was to feel powerless to change things – to long for change and for it not to happen. I think we owe it to ourselves to become really clear about what our needs are. If our needs are not being met, we have every right to ask for change. And if change doesn't come, then I guess we just have to realise we have a choice.

Don't push things under the rug, even though it is easy to do. Recognise and identify the abuse. Once you have done that, get help to confront it. Don't make it your fault or problem. It's his problem, from way back. You didn't start his problems; you inherited them.

It is really important to take some time out to think things over. If possible, go away for at least a weekend and really focus on yourself from all angles: physically, emotionally, mentally and spiritually. I know from my own experience that by taking some time and focusing within, the answers about what to do will come.

If I could go back to the beginning I'd tackle the problems as soon as I saw them arising. I wouldn't just let them go. And although I'd try to work things out for a reasonable amount of time, I wouldn't hang in there for twenty-five years again, kids or no kids. Nothing much was accomplished by staying so long. My adult family all feel now that they had a hard time. I am not suggesting anyone leave at the first row. But for heaven's sake don't let yourself be put down. We don't have to feel inferior.

Pull right back and take some time to reflect. Write letters to yourself about what is happening, what you want from the relationship and whether you actually want to stay or go. Think about how much the relationship means to you and what you really think of that other person. Find out how you feel and where you want to go in your life.

I'd really advise women to stand back and ask themselves the question my counsellor asked me, 'Is this how someone who says he loves me should treat me?' When I considered that question, it was a real breakthrough.

If you want the relationship to work and you believe it can, then set the wheels of change in motion. Find out if your partner is prepared to go to counselling. If he does, remember it takes a very strong and courageous person to change. It has to be worked at all the time, not just for three or four token sessions with a counsellor. Although it may sound hard, if your partner is not prepared to work at it, then you may as well leave now, because in my experience it doesn't get any better.

If you want to leave, you can do it. It is possible. You need to take one step at a time, and the first step may be to pick up the phone and to tell someone, 'I need help.' I'm a volunteer for the Women's Refuge now, and we are there to support any woman that is in an abusive relationship. Don't be afraid to talk to someone about what's happening.

If you are living with any form of abuse, don't put up with it any longer. If he won't change, I advise you to get out. That's not easy to do, I know, but for your own sake and the sake of your children, don't put up with it. You may think the children are not affected, but they do remember and it has a dramatic effect on them in the years to come.

You're a person, an individual with your own rights and your own feelings. Don't allow yourself to be robbed of your self-esteem, your individuality, and your compassion and love.

Realise you do have a choice. For a long time I never thought I did. When I realised I could choose, I was able to stop giving my power away to my partner and take it back for me.

I'd hate to see women put themselves through the years and years of absolute horror that I put myself and my children through. My best advice to anyone is to talk to people about what is happening. I don't think any woman should put up with anyone abusing her. Look at the reasons you are letting that happen to you. Have a really long look. It really would have helped if I had done that.

I'd say if it's bad, don't stay, because it is damaging. I'm forty-six and I think that generation tends to stick things out too long. I feel you've got nothing to gain by sticking it out. It's just not worth it. My life is completely different now: nothing special, but I can be myself and do what I like. Getting to know myself again has been important. And just being happy and always laughing like I used to be before I was married.

You can't change your partner. For a long time I thought I could. It took me too many years of abuse to realise that the only one I could change is me. If I wanted change, then I had to instigate it. I had to be the one to make myself and my children safe, and start again. Once I decided to go, it was not nearly as difficult as it had seemed.

You can get out if you want to. There is hope. But it's up to you. Only you can do it. I know what it feels like to be too scared to go. People would tell me to get out, but for a long time I couldn't. I'm remarried now and it's so different. I can do whatever I want. I can go to the gym and sit down at night and relax. I can be myself, and my husband just accepts me the way I am. I didn't know it could be like this. I've watched other women struggling in bad relationships and it's hard to make them believe that it really is possible to rebuild your life.

If you want to leave, don't put it off. I was married for forty-three years and was nearly seventy when I finally got out. I'll regret to my dying day that I waited so long. By the time my husband left I was addicted to tranquillisers and was in a total zombie state. After he'd gone I cried day and night, not because he'd left but because of what he'd done to me and all the life I'd lost. Now I'm going to study matrimonial law so I can help other people. After what I've learnt in the last two years, I'm halfway there already!

You can cope on your own if you have to. I'd never wish a break-up on anyone, especially if there are children involved, but sometimes it's the only way. It's amazing how little money you can survive on if you have to. We may not do a lot of things, but we are all healthy and I'm managing to pay the bills, and quite frankly we have been a damn sight happier as a family unit. We have stuck together and all of us have changed for the better. People who see me now can't get over the difference. They used to think I was such a little mouse. I've got so much more confidence now.

Don't be afraid to leave because of the children. Bringing up children on your own can be a really positive experience. Since we've been on our own, the children have been able to do things they never would have done if Mike had stayed. Seeing them today is really satisfying. It hasn't always been easy. I've had to work very hard, and we've had our ups and downs, but when you succeed against the odds you know you've really succeeded. So, out of a negative situation, positive things can come.

Listen very carefully to what's going on inside you and what your little voice is telling you. Don't ignore those basic gut feelings like I did for so long. I didn't really want to face leaving because I was so afraid of how I'd cope alone. But it's not as hard as you think. I put off the inevitable, and now I think, 'Why did I leave it so long?' Now everything is absolutely wonderful. I feel as if I'm coming alive again. Women need to know that being on your own can be really good.

Don't attempt an amicable separation without the help of a solicitor. You may wake up five years down the track and realise that your partner used your fear and willingness to please to cheat you, probably at the same time as you were being grateful to him for not being as mean as you expected him to be.

I think finding out more about what happens to women in our society can really make you more aware of what's happening in the relationship. Feminism has made me realise that we are not just talking about one couple, we are talking about a social issue here. Feminism has gradually given me the right to be indignant. At first I could only feel that indignation on other women's behalf. Only now, six years down the track, am I beginning to feel indignant on my own behalf.

One thing I know for sure is that when we are silent about what is happening, we give our partner power. As long as we are silent we'll continue to be isolated, so speak out and get support.

When you're in the relationship you have no idea of how it feels to be free. When I finally did say, 'I'm out of here', I felt such independence. After that taste of freedom, I'd never go back. I can do what I like. Even though I live in a grotty flat at the moment, the world is my oyster. I'm so much more positive now.

No matter how impossible it seems now, you can create a new life for yourself. Just hang on to the belief that it is possible. I used to think that I'd never have a life that was worth living again. I thought it was just too hard to let go and start again, but I was wrong. It's been a challenge, but I have a wonderful new life, new dreams, friends and things I'm involved in. Life is definitely worth living. I hope women can believe that, and find the strength to make a new start if they have to.

It's never too late to start again. I was in my fifties when I left and I was scared, but in the end it was a matter of saving my sanity. Now six years after leaving I'm still on my own. If I'd envisaged this then, I'd have been pretty blue, but actually I'm quite content. There's so much of interest to get involved in. If I got into another relationship I'd have to give up too much; I'd never have the time to do it all. Nowadays I can please myself how much I do for my kids and grandkids, and I have marvellous friends. We have such good times together going out to films and shows.

Hold on to what's really important to you. The one thing that kept me going and stopped me from killing myself was that I believed in myself as a woman. Women have been around for a long time, and women are survivors. It doesn't matter what has happened to them, women do survive. And that one little skinny thread was the thing that I kept hanging on to. The thing that kept me going was my woman-ness. That was my lifeline. That was my sanity.

Compared to how it was, my life now is heaven. I definitely have peace of mind. I feel calm and sane and I know who I am. It's just paradise.

Appendix One

For Family and Friends

- Offer the woman who is in an abusive relationship the gift of a listening ear and an accepting heart. Usually the woman is terribly ashamed of her situation, so if she finds the courage to confide in you she deserves your respect. It is important to let her know you understand her dilemma and you do not judge her. The woman needs to know that you believe her story, no matter how unlikely it seems and how caring and kind her partner appears. Although it can be tempting to maintain a neutral position rather than taking sides, you need to consider that by remaining an impartial observer you are indirectly supporting the more powerful partner. The woman needs someone on her side to help redress the power imbalance.

- Let the woman know you care. Offer her any help you are willing to give. She may appreciate child-care, regular phone contact and visits, or the offer of a place to stay or the loan of money if she is thinking of leaving. She might also like help in finding out about community resources like a women's support group, women's refuges, income support services or emergency housing. Ask the woman what she wants of you and give it to her if you can. In fact your compassionate listening and reassurance about her worth and sanity may be all that she needs from you at that time.

- Acknowledge your limitations. If you offer more of yourself than you are able to give, you may end up feeling resentful and unable to give any support at all. Let the woman know how much you can do to help and if you feel you cannot give the woman what she needs at that time tell her so. You may then be able to offer a time when you can meet that need, or help her to work out a way to achieve the same thing without your help.

- Find ways to take care of yourself. Supporting a person in distress can be very demanding and may evoke powerful feelings in you. You may feel anxious, overwhelmed, discouraged, appalled, distressed, impatient, helpless, angry or frightened. You may experience the discomfort of divided loyalties, the heartbreak of being unable to prevent the suffering of someone you care about, or the frustration of your opinion not being acted on. It is important for your well-being to acknowledge and express these feelings to a neutral person.

- The way you respond to the woman's story is vitally important. Beware of implying the abuse is the woman's fault by asking what she did to upset her partner or focusing on her past history of abuse as a reason for what is happening now. Instead, encourage the woman to tell you about how her partner is behaving toward her, and how that makes her feel. Let her know that you can be trusted to respect her confidentiality.

- Help the woman to see that the abuse is not her fault. She does not need to strive for perfection in the hope of pleasing her partner. It is not her responsibility to keep him calm and satisfied. It is his choice if he becomes angry, drunk or abusive, and she cannot change this behaviour. Remind her that the excuses her partner gives for his destructive behaviour do not justify his abuse. He has no right to abuse her.

- If you are concerned about the women's safety let her know this. Help her to decide what she will do, where she will go and how she will get there if her safety is threatened. Make sure she has the phone number for the local women's refuge and realises that they offer a safe, confidential place to go. Also remind her she can phone the police if her safety is at risk.

- Encourage the woman to maintain close links with friends and family and pursue interests outside the home. The more isolated the woman is, the more demoralised she is likely to become and the more control her partner will gain. Contact with people who treat her well helps to boost her diminishing self-esteem. Encourage the woman to have time out from her children if this is possible. Both the woman and her children will benefit from this.

- Accept the woman's feelings of confusion about her partner. She may still love him. There are probably still happy moments as well as distressing ones. Her hope of a happy future may be rekindled many times. The woman usually copes by denying the existence of abuse or minimising its impact. Sometimes the woman will express her feeling of outrage at her partner's mistreatment then later seem to have forgotten what took place. She may say the abuse was not so bad and her partner has now changed. This is all part of the process of coming to terms with her situation. It can be helpful to remind the woman gently of the past destructive episodes, but be cautious about criticising the man. This can put the woman in the position of defending him.

- Don't assume the woman's situation is straightforward or that it is easy to leave a partner who is abusive. There are many fears to be faced, practical decisions to be made and ties to be broken before the woman can separate. Ironically the more abusive her partner becomes, the more difficult the woman may find it to leave him. This is because the woman's self-esteem, confidence and strength are being continually undermined, until eventually she has little faith in her ability to cope alone.

- The woman may not be ready to accept your offers of help at the time they are first offered. She may be locked into denial about her partner's behaviour, or may be still striving to make the relationship work. Be prepared to wait. Although your offer of help may not be taken up at the time, the woman may hold on to that offer through the bad times, and it may be the lifeline that helps her to take action some time later. The most vital point is that the woman knows that you will be there if she needs you.

- As you walk beside the woman on this journey, a great deal of patience may be demanded of you. She may need to talk about what is happening numerous times and make many attempts to improve her situation before she is able to consider leaving. If her partner is constantly blaming her for the abuse and invalidating her reality, she may need to be reminded often that she is a sane person who other people love and care about and she is entitled to a peaceful life.

- You will probably have strong beliefs about what the woman 'should' do, but it is important not to impose these on her. If the woman wants your opinion it is appropriate to give it, but ultimately you need to respect her right to make her own decisions and allow her time to do this. If a woman does not appear to be capable of deciding what to do, it can be tempting to take over. But when she is forced to make a move before she is ready, the woman often returns to the relationship. This can leave you feeling frustrated and reluctant to assist her again. If the woman does require active support to help leave, be sure to step back and allow her to regain full control of her life as soon as possible.

- If the woman is wanting to leave and is considering going to a women's refuge, think carefully before you intervene with an offer of temporary accommodation. Staying with a family member is not always the best decision. It usually means that the woman's partner has access to her and his pressure may cause her to return home. At the refuge the woman will have input from skilled workers who will be able to advise her on the procedure for obtaining court orders and custody of the children, and give her information about the dynamics of abuse which will empower her in the future.

- If the woman does separate from her partner, avoid acting as a go-between. Informing the woman of her partner's actions, threats or promises places an extra stress on her. Her partner's actions are not her responsibility. Nor is she in a position to do anything about them. Her priority is the rebuilding of her own life.

- When a woman chooses to return to a destructive relationship it can be deeply distressing for those supporting her. At this time it can be helpful to hold on to the fact that although this may happen a number of times, each time she leaves she gains a little strength and clarity. Given enough support the day will come when she is able to reclaim her power within the relationship or leave for the final time. Your support is as vital as a heartbeat.

Appendix Two

For Counsellors and Other Professionals

- If you suspect a woman client is being abused, it is usually better to see her alone rather than with her partner. This gives the woman the opportunity to be honest about her situation without fear of her partner's retaliation. If joint counselling is undertaken, be aware that the controlling man often presents very plausibly as charming, caring and at ease while the woman may be anxious and unresponsive.

- Women in abusive relationships may display symptoms of depression, anxiety, alcoholism, drug addiction or other stress-related illnesses. It is important to consider the woman's symptoms in the context of her situation and look beyond these symptoms for the cause. For instance, the woman with post-natal depression may be distressed about her partner's aggressive reactions to having a new baby in the house and despondent about her future. Try asking questions that focus on the partner's behaviour like: 'What does your partner do if the baby cries at night?' or 'How does he react if you don't want to have sex?' Avoid labelling the woman. Labels stick and can become just another part of the abuse.

- It is easy to overlook abuse because many women do not realise that their partner is emotionally or sexually abusing them. They tend to believe his claim that their failure to perform to his standards is justification for his destructive behaviour. This often makes the woman feel guilty, ashamed and driven to try harder to please her partner. As she adapts to his controlling behaviour the woman often loses sight of how inappropriate and destructive her partner's behaviour is. Help her to identify this behaviour as abusive and try gently reminding her this is not the way men treat their partners in healthy relationships.

- Assist the woman in assessing her safety. Help her to decide what she will do and where she will go if her safety is threatened. Give her the phone number of the local women's refuge and explain their services to her. If you are concerned for her safety, tell her so.

- Most women who are suffering abuse develop low self-esteem. In their attempts to cope some will have adopted behaviour that has become self-defeating. Many women fear they are going crazy. It is important to remember that the woman's symptoms are the result of the abuse *not* the cause of it. Assist the woman in realising this. Reassure her frequently that she is not going crazy.

- Give the woman information about the dynamics of abuse and the impact this has on women's self-esteem and health. Inform her that behind incidents of abuse are issues of power and control. Help her to identify what her partner gains through the abusive episodes and put her experience into a wider social and historical context. Let her know she is not alone. Woman abuse is a common problem in our society.

- Believe the woman even if her stories sound contradictory. Women usually cope with the abuse they are suffering by denial and minimising. As the woman comes out of denial her recall of events may be clouded and fragmented. It may be quite a time before she can overcome her feelings of shame and confusion to talk about the most traumatic incidents. It takes courage for the woman to share her painful truth. She needs to know that you accept and respect her as a person.

- Despite her partner's control tactics the woman may still have strong feelings for him. Between episodes of abuse there may be times of calmness and love which renew the woman's hope for change. Help her to work through her feelings of confusion and ambivalence about her partner. She will need time to come to terms with these feelings so she can come to a decision about what to do in the future.

- Don't say or imply that the woman is responsible for provoking her partner's abuse. Irrespective of what the woman has done, it is the man's responsibility if he abuses. And remember that although women can and do emotionally abuse men, this does not have the same power to generate fear because it is usually not accompanied by the threat of physical or sexual abuse.

- Don't join the woman in her search for reasons for her partner's abuse. This search keeps her hoping for a magical solution rather than facing the facts and deciding what to do about them. Assist the woman in shifting the focus off her partner and on to herself.

- Realise the woman is probably not in a position to negotiate with her partner. Abuse is not a question of communication or lack of assertiveness. It is an issue of power and control. Don't assume that if the woman becomes more assertive her partner will back off and treat her with respect. Most controlling men will increase their abusive behaviour if their partner takes a stand. At this stage the woman may be at risk. Her attempts at reclaiming her power need to be taken in small planned steps with plenty of support.

- Help the woman to break out of isolation. People and interests outside the home are her lifeline. Encourage her to maintain contact with her friends and family and build a support network. In conjunction with your work, refer her to a group for women living in abusive relationships. These groups provide invaluable support, information and new perspectives. Being part of a group helps the woman overcome her feelings of shame and isolation.

- Giving the woman a task to do between sessions can be a helpful means of empowering her to regain control over her life. The early tasks need to be achievable small steps that will not put her at risk, such as phoning a friend or finding out about a support group.

- If the woman is considering separation, help her to explore the various options and work through the practical problems she will face. Remember that the abusive man is usually quite dependent on his partner, so her decision to leave could place her safety at risk. This may need to be addressed and safety strategies decided on.

- Remind the woman constantly that she is not to blame for

the abuse, nor does she deserve to be mistreated. She is entitled to a safe and happy life. She cannot change her partner, nor prevent his abuse if he is determined to mistreat her. If he does change, it will be because he has decided to. Although she has no power over that decision, the woman does have the power to change herself and her own life.

Appendix Three

Obtaining Court Orders

There are various types of court orders available. The following information is intended only as a guide. You will need to consult a lawyer to decide what action you should take in your particular situation.

Under the present law, the orders available are essentially non-molestation and occupation orders. They can be issued in any of the courts that deal with family law issues. This means you can apply either to a Family Proceedings Court where magistrates will consider the application or to a District judge or Circuit judge in the County Courts and where appropriate to a High Court judge if a case is to be heard there. These orders can be applied for when there is fear for the safety of a woman and/or children. In many cases she will have been physically harmed by her partner at least once and be considered to be in danger of being harmed again. Sometimes verbal or emotional abuse or threats are sufficient reason for an order to be granted. These orders should be obtained soon after any abusive episode.

Non-molestation orders
Obtaining a non-molestation order against your partner prohibits him from making contact with you or coming near you without your permission. This may include visiting your home or following you, phoning you, or contacting you or your children. If your partner breaks this order he can either be arrested, if a power of arrest is attached to the order, or, where no power of arrest is attached, he can be committed to prison for breaking this injunction. If arrested under a power of arrest then your partner would be brought before the court within 24 hours of any arrest and the matter considered further by the court. He can be committed to prison for a period of time where appropriate.

238* *Invisible Wounds*

A warrant can also be issued if no power of arrest is attached to the order. If arrested on a warrant your partner can be released on bail or remanded in custody when he is brought before the court.

You can obtain this order even if you are living under the same roof and a power of arrest can be attached where there has been violence used against you or your child.

Occupation orders
In addition to non-molestation orders, the court can also suspend any rights of occupation that your partner has entitling them to remain living in the home with a further order that your partner may have to leave the home and not return to the home for a specified period. These are usually seen as short-term remedies which can run for up to six months. A court may in certain circumstances be able to consider excluding your partner from a specified area of the home.

The Protection from Harassment Act 1997 is also available when either crime or criminal jurisdiction is involved.

Assault and/or trespass orders
If neither you or your partner are living together or have been living together for some time, then the present legislation dealing with domestic violence may not be applicable. In those circumstances, if there has been an assault upon you, or if your partner has come to your home without your permission and caused damage, then an application to the County Court under the civil law for assault and/or trespass will have to be considered. These orders can be made in a County Court for the area in which you reside and will be made in accordance with the merits of the case. These applications are claims for damages together with an injunction although as the essence of these proceedings is protection, the claim for damages is often not pursued. A power of arrest cannot be attached to this order and will have to be enforced by a further application for commital if there is a breach of the order.

How to obtain an appropriate order
Go to a lawyer who is experienced in family law. He or she will take down your statement (affidavit) detailing any threats or

assaults by your partner. Be as accurate as possible with the details of the dates, times and place of the assault, the injuries and how any threats were delivered. Give your lawyer the medical notes for any treatment you have received for injuries.

After you have signed the affidavit your lawyer will present it to the judge. If you believe your safety is immediately at risk, you can ask for the application to be made 'ex parte' – that is, without any notice to your partner. Although there must be serious concerns for your safety for the order to be granted on an ex parte basis, judges are usually quite willing to grant these orders. If an order is made, it comes into effect immediately it is served on your partner. From the time you visit your lawyer to the time a judge makes an order can be as little as a few hours.

This ex parte order is a temporary measure. When the judge grants this interim order he or she will set a date for review. At that time your partner can defend the order by claiming he is not a threat to you. Some men do not bother trying to defend the orders, so final orders can be made at the review date.

The other way to obtain an order is 'on notice'. This means the relevant court documents are served on your partner and he has the right to defend himself in court after reading your affidavit before the order is granted. This usually takes a week or two.

When your order has a power of arrest attached make sure your solicitor gives a copy of it to the local police after it has been served. Also make sure you have a copy as soon as the order is granted, even if it has not yet been served upon your partner. Remember, the order will only become effective once it has been served upon your partner.

It is up to you to reinforce this order by consistently phoning the police every time your partner attempts to make contact. This way your partner is given a very clear message: you will not tolerate his abuse. Your order is only as effective as the consistent follow-up you initiate.

Legal aid

If you are in a lower income bracket, you will probably qualify for legal aid for payment of your legal costs. Depending on your financial circumstances, you may have to pay a contribution. Your fees may be paid in full if you do not have savings or own property. If you own property, you may be required to repay the amount of legal aid granted when you sell this property. The possibility of being granted legal aid, the conditions that apply and whether you may have to repay legal aid should be discussed with your lawyer on your first visit.

Provided by David McHardy LL.B of Hutchins & Co., Solicitors, London.

Appendix Four

The Women and Their Stories

Although the stereotype of the abused woman is still of a masochistic and helpless victim, this is not the reality. Women who live through abusive relationships are strong survivors. While writing this book I have endeavoured to honour that resilience, strength and courage.

Fifty women were interviewed in depth for the purpose of gathering first-hand accounts of emotional abuse. Throughout this book, their words vividly express what this experience meant to them. The women ranged in age from 23 to 73. I found the women at random, simply by asking people I knew if they could put me in touch with a woman who had experienced an emotionally abusive relationship. Those women then put me in touch with others. The surprising ease of networking 50 women in this way shows just how common and yet invisible this problem is. I also interviewed a thirteen-year-old girl, to gain insights into living in an emotionally abusive situation from a child's point of view. All names and any identifying characteristics of the women and their children and partners have been changed to protect their identity.

A small minority of the women interviewed had suffered physical as well as emotional abuse. Several of these women commented that they found the emotional violence more painful and destructive than the physical. Generally the impact is very similar for both types of abuse.

The information I gathered was never intended to be a piece of research, but it is important to note that several common factors presented repeatedly. The main recurring patterns were:

- The man's abusive behaviour increased over time.
- The woman tended to try to cope with her partner's moods and demands by compliance.

- As a result of the increasing stress, the woman experienced a deterioration in her mental and physical health.

Other similarities were:
- Many of the women described their partners as charming and intelligent men who could at times be delightful companions. This tended to keep the women confused about the reality of their situation and hoping for positive change.
- Most women did not clearly label their partner's behaviour as abusive while they were in the relationship, but they can identify it as such in retrospect.
- The controlling man tended to justify his abusive behaviour by citing the woman's failure to meet his needs, keep the house, manage the finances or perform to his standards in a multitude of other ways.
- Most women believed their partner's claim that they were to blame for his bad behaviour.
- The women did not accept the abuse passively but were remarkably resourceful in trying to find new ways to stem the flow or to cope with the abuse.
- As they looked back on their relationship, many of the women experienced a sense of unreality and sometimes horror at what they had lived through. At some stage almost all doubted their sanity. Most experienced depression; many were on medication; several were seeing psychiatrists; some had panic attacks, breakdowns, suicidal thoughts or had attempted suicide; three were diagnosed with a mental illness; and one was referred for shock treatment. Once out of the relationship, all regained their mental health with surprising speed. From their more peaceful and happier present lives, they find it difficult to reconcile those memories with how they view themselves today.
- All of the women stayed in their relationship for several years. Although they felt at the time that staying was the right decision, many now express regret at the lost years and wish they had left sooner.
- Many of the women are now aware of the way in which their female conditioning led them to take far too much responsibility for the relationship, kept them striving to please and blinded them to the reality of their partner's abuse.

All but three of the women are now living apart from their abusive partners. Although many regretted the fact that their partner's behaviour made it necessary to leave, none regretted their decision to create a new life for themselves. All are glad to be free from the heartbreak of that time.

Appendix Five

Community Resources

There are many organisations which offer support, information and assistance. The following list covers some of them. If these organisations cannot offer you the kind of support you need, ask them to recommend another that may be suitable.

Community information
The Citizens Advice Bureaux are excellent sources of information about local social service agencies, support groups, courses, legal rights, housing, welfare and health issues. The CAB also offer a free legal advice service in many areas (by appointment) and a free budgeting service. Check your local directory for the phone number.

Phone lines
A 24-hour phone counselling service is operated by the Samaritans. Rape crisis centres offer a phone line to survivors of rape or sexual abuse. The phone numbers for these organisations are listed below.

Women's Aid
A network offering safe, confidential accommodation to women who are leaving an abusive relationship, along with their children. They provide support, information and practical assistance. The contact numbers are listed below.

Counselling
Check the 'Counselling Services' section of the Yellow Pages or contact your Citizens Advice Bureau for information, or contact the counselling services listed below.

Community mental health
Many hospitals have special mental health units where free counselling is offered to people who are suffering emotional

distress and mental health problems. To find out if this service is available in your area phone your local hospital or check the 'Hospital' section in the front of your phone directory for 'Mental Health Services'.

Alcohol and drug addiction
Most hospitals have a special unit which offers free assessment, support and counselling for people who are experiencing a problem with substance abuse. To find out if this service is available in your area, phone your local hospital or check the 'Hospital' section in the front of your local directory for 'Alcohol and Drug Services'. If this service is not available, ask the hospital to recommend another source of assistance.

Alcoholics Anonymous (AA) offer a confidential, nationwide network of support groups for people with a drinking problem. Payment for these groups is by donation. The phone numbers for these services will be in your local phone directory.

Child abuse
Social services are responsible for the care and protection of children and young people. Their role is to investigate all reports of neglect or child abuse and to work with the family to find solutions that are in the interests of the child. Check your local phone directory for the number of your social services department.

Sexual abuse
Rape crisis groups have well-trained people who offer support and counselling to survivors of sexual abuse and rape. The phone numbers for these organisations are listed below by area. Other local organisations that specialise in this field may be listed under 'Counselling Services' in your Yellow Pages.

Women's support groups
Some areas have special support groups for women who are living in or recovering from abusive relationships. Check your local CAB to see if there is a women's group near you. Women's general support groups are often offered by women's centres and local community houses. Other courses on confidence building, self-assertion, women's spirituality, parenting or many other self-development topics may be available through your

local adult education classes. Check with the CAB.

If your partner has a problem with substance abuse, Al-Anon run support groups.

Income support and other benefits
For specific details phone your branch of the Employment Service.

Counselling and therapy

British Association of Psychotherapists
37 Mapesbury Road
London NW2 4HJ
Tel 020 8452 9823

British Association of Counselling
1 Regent Place
Rugby
Warks
Tel 01788 578 328

Scottish Association of Counselling
26 Frederick Street
Edinburgh
EH2 2JH

Northern Ireland Association of Counselling
93 Laharna Avenue
Larne
BT40 lNY

Jewish Marriage Counselling
MIYAD Crisis Line
Tel 020 8203 6211/0345 581 999

Asian Family Counselling Service
74 The Avenue
London W13 8LB
Tel 020 8567 5616

Women's Therapy Centre
10 Manor Gardens
London N7 6JS
Tel 020 7263 6200 (advice)/020 7263 7860 (business line)

Mind
Headquarters
Granta House
15–19 Broadway
Stratford
London E15 4BQ
Tel 020 8519 2122
Mental health information and advice, and support groups.
Check in your Yellow Pages or with the operator for your local
service.

Relate
Herbert Gray College
Little Church Street
Rugby
Warks CV21 3AP
Tel 01788 573241
Formerly Marriage Guidance Association

Release
388 Old Street
London
ECIV 9LT
Tel 020 7729 9904
Help with addiction

Samaritans
Tel 0345 90 90 90 (national help line)
Email jo@samaritans.org.uk
Check in your Yellow Pages or with the operator for your local
service.

Legal advice and mediation

Solicitors Family Law Association
PO Box 302
Orpington
Kent
BR6 8QX
Tel 01689 850227
They will put you in touch with a solicitor specialising in dealing with family law.

National Association of Citizens Advice Bureaux
115–123 Pentonville Road
London
N1 9LZ
Tel 020 7833 2181

Rights of Women
52–54 Featherstone Street
London
EC1Y 8RT
Tel 020 7251 6577
Offer information and advice to women.

The National Council for One Parent Families
255 Kentish Town Road
London
NW5 2LX
Tel 020 7267 1361 (business)/0800 018 5026 (helpline)

Family Welfare Association
501–505 Kingsland High Road
London
E8 4AU
Tel 020 7254 6251
Offer support for people experiencing family and relationship problems.

National Family Mediation
9 Tavistock Place
London
WC1H 9SN
Tel 020 7383 5993
Will put you in touch with a family mediation service near you.

Cambridge Family and Divorce Centre
Essex House
71 Regent Street
Cambridge
CB2 1AB
Tel 01223 576 308
Provide a range of services from legal information to mediation.

Women's Aid

Women's Aid Federation England
PO Box 391
Bristol
BS99 7WS
Tel 0117 9444411/0345 023 468

Northern Ireland Women's Aid
129 University Street
Belfast
BT7 1HP
Tel 00353 1874 5302/3

Scottish Women's Aid
13/9 North Bank Street
Edinburgh
EH1 2LN
Tel 0131 229 1419

Welsh Women's Aid – Aberystwyth
2nd Floor
12 Cambrian Place
Aberystwyth

Dyfed
SY23 1NT
Tel 01970 612748

Welsh Women's Aid – Cardiff
38–48 Crwys Road
Cardiff
CF2 4NN
Tel 029 3920 0874

Welsh Women's Aid – Rhyl
1st Floor
26 Wellington Road
Rhyl
Clwyd
LL18 IBN
Tel 01745 334767

Rape Crisis Centres

England
Andover Rape Crisis Helpline 01264 336 222
Avon Sexual Abuse Centre 0177 935 1707
Aylesbury Rape Crisis Line 01296 392 468
Basingstoke Rape Crisis 01256 840 224
Bradford Rape Crisis 01724 308 270
Brighton Rape Crisis 01273 203 773
Bucks Rape Crisis 01908 691 969
Cambridge Rape Crisis Centre 01223 358 314
Chelmsford Rape and Sexual Abuse Counselling Centre
01245 492 123
Chester Rape Crisis Centre 01244 317 922
Colchester Rape Crisis Line 01206 769 795
Cornwall Rape and Sexual Abuse Helpline 01872 262 100
Coventry Rape Crisis and Sexual Abuse Counselling
024 7667 7229
Cumbria Rape Crisis 01228 365 002
Derby Rape Crisis 01332 372 545
(Derby) One in Four (young women) 01332 666 274

Doncaster Rape and Sexual Abuse Counselling 01302 360 421
Durham County Rape Crisis Centre 01325 369 933
East Dorset Rape Crisis Line 01202 433 950
East Kent Rape Line 01227 450 400
Exeter Women's Aid Rape Crisis Line 01392 430 871
(Guildford) Rape and Sexual Abuse Centre 01483 454 547
Halton Rape Crisis Group 0151 423 4192
(Hertfordshire) Rape Crisis and Sexual Abuse Line
01923 241 600
Herts Area Rape Crisis 0171 727 6512
Hull Rape Crisis Centre 01482 329 990
(Kent) Sanctuary 01634 378 300
Kirklees Rape Crisis 01484 450 040
Leeds Rape Crisis 01132 441 323
Leicester Rape Crisis Centre 0166 270 6990
London Rape Crisis 020 7837 1600
Luton and District Rape Crisis Centre 01582 33592
Manchester Rape Crisis 0161 834 8784
(North Staffordshire and South Staffordshire) Rape Crisis
01782 204 177
Norwich Rape Crisis 0191 261 7643
Nottingham Rape Crisis Centre 0115 941 0440
Oxford Sexual Abuse and Rape Crisis Centre 01865 726 295
Peterborough Rape Counselling Group 01733 340 515
Plymouth Rape Crisis Line 01752 223584
Portsmouth Area Rape Crisis Service 023 9266 9513
Sandwell Rape Crisis 0121 525 9981
Scunthorpe Rape Crisis 01724 853 953
Sheffield Rape and Sexual Abuse Counselling Service
0114 244 7936
Shropshire Rape Crisis Centre 01952 248 444
South Cumbria Rape and Abuse Service 01539 734 743
South Essex Rape and Incest Crisis Centre 01357 380 609
Southampton Rape Crisis and Sexual Abuse Counselling
023 8070 1213
Southend Rape and Sexual Abuse Support Line
01702 347 933
Suffolk Rape Crisis 01473 715 333
Swindon Rape Crisis 01973 879 280

Thurrock Rape Crisis Centre 01375 380 609
Tyneside Rape Crisis Centre 0191 222 0272
Watford Rape Crisis and Sexual Abuse Line 01923 241 600
Wirral Rape Crisis 0151 666 1392
Worcestershire Rape and Sexual Abuse Support Centre
01905 424 282
Wycombe Rape Crisis Centre 01904 610 917

Scotland
Aberdeen Rape Crisis 01224 620 772
Ayr Rape Crisis Centre and Incest Support 01292 611 301
(Ayrshire) Rape Counselling and Resource Centre
01563 541 769
Dundee Rape Crisis Centre 01382 201 291 (young women's
project 206 222)
Edinburgh Rape Crisis Centre 0131 556 9437
Fife Rape Crisis 01592 650 188
Highland Rape and Abuse Line 01349 865 316
(Rosshire) Rape and Abuse Line 01349 862 686
Shakti Women's Aid (for black and ethnic minority women)
0131 557 4010
Strathclyde Rape Crisis Centre 0141 331 1990
Western Isles Women's Aid 01851 704 750

Wales
(Bangor) Rape Crisis Line 01248 354 885
(Cardiff) Rape Crisis Line 029 2037 3181

Ireland
Northern
Belfast Rape Crisis and Sexual Abuse Centre 028 9024 9696

Republic
Cork Rape Crisis 00353 2196 8086
(Dublin) Rape Crisis Centre 1800 778 888
Galway Rape Crisis 1850 355 355
Limerick Rape Crisis Centre 00353 6131 1511
Waterford Rape Crisis Centre 1800 296 296

Bibliography

I would like to gratefully acknowledge the following books and warmly recommend them as further reading.

Woman abuse
Forward, Susan, *Men Who Hate Women and the Women Who Love Them: When loving hurts and you don't know why*, London, Bantam, 1988
Hite, Shere and Colleran, Kate, *Good Guys Bad Guys and Other Lovers*, London, Pandora, 1991
Horley, Sandra, *Love and Pain: A survival handbook for women*, London, Bedford Square Press, 1988
Horley, Sandra, *The Charm Syndrome: Why charming men can make dangerous lovers*, London, Macmillan, 1991
NiCarthy, Ginny, *Getting Free. A handbook for women in abusive relationships*, Washington, The Seal Press, 1990
Porterfield, Kay Marie, *What's a Nice Girl Like You Doing in a Relationship Like This?* California, Journeyman, 1992

Sexual abuse
Bass, Ellen and Laura, Davis, *The Courage to Heal: A guide for women survivors of child sexual abuse*, New York, Cedar, 1990
Davis, Laura, *The Courage to Heal Workbook: For women and men survivors of child sexual abuse*, London, Mandarin, 1990
Saphira, Miriam, *For Your Child's Sake: Understanding sexual abuse*, New Zealand, Heinemann Reid, 1987

Mental Health
Bloomfield, Harold, and McWilliams, Peter, *How to Heal Depression*, London, Thorsons, 1995
Braiker, Harriet, *Getting Up When You're Feeling Down: A woman's guide to overcoming and preventing depression*, London, Robson Books, 1989

Firth-Cozens, Jenny, *Nervous Breakdown*, London, Piaktus, 1988

Markham, Ursula, *Women and Guilt: How to set aside your feelings of guilt and lead a positive life*, London, Piaktus, 1995

McCormick, Elizabeth Wilde, *Nervous Breakdown: A positive guide to coping, healing and rebuilding*, London, Unwin Hyman, 1988

Alcoholism

Hodgkinson, Liz, *Alcoholism: Your questions answered*, London, Ward Lock, 1995

Kessel, Neil, and Walton, Henry, *Alcoholism*, London, Penguin, 1993

Self-Esteem

Branden, Nathaniel, *The Power of Self-Esteem: An inspiring look at our most important psychological resource*, Pompano Beach, Health Communications, 1992

Butler, Pamela, *Self-Assertion for Women*, San Francisco, Harper & Row, 1992

Field, Lynda, *Creating Self-Esteem: A practical guide to realizing your true worth*, Dorset, Element Books, 1993

Field, Lynda, *The Self-Esteem Workbook: An interactive process to changing your life*, Dorset, Element Books, 1993

Hillman, Carolynn, *Recovery of Your Self-Esteem: A guide for women*, New York, Simon & Schuster, 1992

Sanford, Linda T, and Donovan, Mary Ellen, *Women and Self-Esteem: Understanding and improving the way we think and feel about ourselves*, London, Penguin, 1993

Thoele, Sue Patton, *The Courage To Be Yourself: A woman's guide to growing beyond emotional dependence*, Berkeley, Conari Press, 1991

Relationships and communication

Forward, Susan, *Obsessive Love: When passion holds you prisoner*, London, Bantam Books, 1991

Hendrix, Harville, *Getting the Love You Want: A guide for couples*, London, Pocket Books, 1993

Lerner, Harriet Goldhor, *The Dance of Anger: A woman's guide to the patterns of intimate relationships*, London, Pandora, 1992

Lindenfield, Gael, *Managing Anger: Positive strategies for dealing with destructive emotions*, London, Thorsons, 1993

Paul, Jordan and Margaret, *Do I Have to Give Up Me to be Loved by You?*, Wellingborough, Grapevine, 1989

Phelps, Stanlee, and Austin, Nancy, *The Assertive Women: A new look*, London, Arlington Books, 1991

Personal growth and inspiration

Dowrick, Stephanie, *Intimacy and Solitude*, London, The Women's Press, 1992

Dowrick, Stephanie, *The Intimacy and Solitude Self-Therapy Book*, London, The Women's Press, 1993

Estes, Clarissa Pinkola, *Women Who Run With The Wolves: Contacting the power of the wild woman*, London, Rider, 1986

Gawain, Shakti, *Creative Visualization*, California, New World Library, 1995

Gawain, Shakti, with Laura King, *Living in the Light: A guide to personal and planetary transformation*, California, New World Library, 1991

Jeffers, Susan, *Feel The Fear and Do It Anyway*, London, Century Hutchinson, 1991

Ray, Sondra, *I Deserve Love: The secrets of a great relationship*, USA, Celestial Arts, 1976

Walker, Alice, *The Color Purple*, London, The Women's Press, 1993

Women and society

Bepko, Claudia, and Krestan, Jo-Ann, *Too Good For Her Own Good: Breaking free from the burden of female responsibility*, New York, HarperCollins, 1991

Dowling, Colette, *The Cinderella Complex: Women's hidden fear of independence*, London, Fontana, 1995

Dowling, Colette, *Perfect Women: Hidden fears of inadequacy and the drive to perform*, London, Collins, 1989

Eichenbaum, Luise, and Orbach, Susie, *What Do Women Want?*, London, HarperCollins, 1994

Miller, Jean Baker, *Towards a New Psychology of Women*, London, Penguin, 1991

Russianoff, Penelope, *Why Do I Think I Am Nothing Without a Man?*, London, Bantam Books, 1983

Healing childhood wounds

Bradshaw, John, *Bradshaw On The Family: A revolutionary way to self-discovery*, Pompano Beach, Health Communications, 1989

Bradshaw, John, *Healing the Shame that Binds You*, Pompano Beach, Health Communications, 1988

Bradshaw, John, *Homecoming: Reclaiming and championing your inner child*, London, Piaktus, 1991

Children

Saphira, Miriam, *For Your Child's Sake: Understanding sexual abuse*, London, Penguin, 1987

Break-up and recovery

Dahl, Tessa, *Working for Love*, London, Michael Joseph, 1988

Fisher, Bruce, *Rebuilding When your relationship ends*, California, Impact, 1992

Peiffer, Vera, *How to Cope with Splitting Up*, London, Sheldon Press, 1991

Index

Abuse
    cycle of,   77–78
    definition of,   24
    excuses/reasons for, 68–72
    faces of,   25–45
    historical context of,   80
    impact of, 465
    myths about,   82–83
    society's role in,   81
    stages of,   75–77
Affirmations,   122, 180
Alcoholics Anonymous
    (A.A.),   102, 245
Al-Anon,   100, 245–46
Alcohol or drug
    addiction,   101–2
Anger (partner's) 38–39,
    44–45, 69–70, 155–66
Anger (yours),   54–55
    acknowledging,   115–1 7
    as a stage of grief,   205–6
    release exercises for,   117

Behaviour (yours)
    impact of abuse on,
    57–60
    self–destructive,   100–1
Beginning experience,
    210–11
Blaming self,   49, 71–72,
    118
Boundaries, 159–60
    See also setting limits
Burn-out, symptoms
    of, 143–44

Change (yours),   150–52,
    163–71
    evaluation of,   171–73
    fear of,   151–52
    partner's resistance
    to,   152–53
    preparing for,   54–55
    See also partner's change
Child abuse
    by your partner,   134–38
    by yourself,   131–32
    definitions of,   134
    See also sexual abuse of
        child
Childhood abuse
    (yours),   65–66
    recovery from,   213–14
Children,
    adaptation of,   128–30
    being set against
        mother,   44
    partner's jealous
        against,   30
    protection of,   130–31,
        134–35, 245–46
    reducing distress of,
        132–34
    symptoms of
        distress,   130
    your inability to cope
        with,   130–32
Co–dependency,   83–84
Coping strategies
    (yours),   57–60
Confiding in others,   96–98

Confronting partner,
    155–56, 163–64, 209–10
Controlling men
    attitudes/beliefs of, 72–74,
        78–79
    behavioural games,
        161–63
    communication
        games, 167
    patterns of
        behaviour, 25–45
    See also partner's change
Counselling, 106–8,
    158–59, 244–45
Court orders, 237–40
Criticism, 37–38
    dealing with, 168–70
Creativity, loss of, 50–51
    reclaiming, 198–99

Depression, 62, 102–5
Distress, symptoms of,
    60–65

Exercise, benefit of, 99, 113
Ex-partner
    completing with,
        202–3, 208–11
    dealing with, 196–97
    reconciling with,
        199–202

Fear, feelings of, 52–53
    facing and
        redefining, 176–78
    of craziness, 35–36, 56
Feelings, 52–56, 66
    importance of, 115
Forgiveness, possibility
    of, 211–12

Goal setting, 98–100,
    214–17
Grief, 193–94, 204–6
    resolution of, 210–11
Guilt, 54

Homicidal feelings, 64

Identity, loss of, 50–52
    rediscovery of after
        break-up, 198–99
Impact of abuse
    on behaviour, 57–60
    on emotions, 52–56
    on health, 60–65
    on identity, 50-52
Inner wisdom, 147–49
Isolation, breaking, 95–100

Medication, 105–6
Myths about abuse, 68–72,
    82–83

Parenting, difficulty
    of, 130–32
Partner's change, 141–42
    help available, 156–59
    measuring, 171
Police, dealing with, 188–89
Power, personal, 109–10,
    154
Problem solving, 178–79

Recovery after
    separation, 204-20
    women's strategies
        for, 217–20
Rights (yours), 51–52,
    160–61

Safety
    after break-up, 197–98
    before break-up, 39,
        144–45, 181–2, 189–90
    court orders, 237–40,
        108
Self, loss of, 50
    relationship with,
        109–10, 198
Self acceptance, 110–11
Self care, 111–14
Self esteem, loss of, 51
    affirmations for, 122
Self talk critical, 118-19
    positive, 119–20
Self-image improving,
    119–21
Separation, 225–28
    barriers to, 89–94
    making decision about,
        140–49
    partner's possible
        reactions to, 183–86
    preparation for, 175–85,
        191
    reconciliation, 199–200
    safety aspects of, 181,
        187, 197–98, 237–38
    early stages of, 193–96
Setting limits, 163–67
    See also boundaries
Sexual abuse (of child),
    135–38

Sexual abuse (of
    women), 39–42, 164–65
Shame, 53–54
Sleep, 35, 103, 113
Spirituality, 108
Stress, release of, 113–14,
    125–26
Suicidal feelings, 103–4
Suicide, partner's threats
    of, 186
Support groups, 100
    for recovery after
        relationship, 206–7,
        210–11
Support, other people's,
    95–96, 132–34
    while separating,
        182–83, 206–7

Thoughts,
    obsessional, 122–24, 208

Wisdom, women's, 120–27
Women,
    and transformational
        love, 87–88
    responsibility for
        relationships, 86
    society's expectations
        of, 54, 845, 130–31
Women's Aid, 183
Writing, 124–25, 207,
    208–9

Established in 1978, The Women's Press publishes high-quality fiction and non-fiction from outstanding women writers worldwide. Our list spans literary fiction, crime thrillers, biography and autobiography, health, women's studies, literary criticism, mind body spirit, the arts and the Livewire Books series for young women. Our bestselling annual *Women Artists Diary* features the best in contemporary women's art.

The Women's Press also runs a book club through which members can buy, every quarter, the best fiction and non-fiction from a wide range of British publishing houses, mostly in paperback, always at discount.

To receive our latest catalogue, or for information on The Women's Press Book Club, send a large SAE to:

The Sales Department
The Women's Press Ltd
34 Great Sutton Street London EC1V 0LQ
Tel: 020 7251 3007 Fax: 020 7608 1938
www.the-womens-press.com

Stephanie Dowrick
Intimacy and Solitude
Balancing Closeness and Independence

Why is it that when we are in intimate relationships, we may
often feel dissatisfied, inadequate and claustrophobic?
But then, once we are on our own, we get lonely and have
difficulties enjoying solitude? In this internationally bestselling
book, Stephanie Dowrick draws on a wide range of personal
experiences, and on psychotherapy's most useful insights,
to show how success in intimacy depends on success in
solitude – and vice versa.

Whether experiencing solitude through choice or through
circumstance, *Intimacy and Solitude* enables us to discover our
own unique inner world – and offers real possibilities for
lasting, positive change.

'Sympathetically, and with a rare clarity, it offers
penetrating insights into some of the most basic
paradoxes of human relationships' *Guardian*

'Essential reading . . . A penetrating, thoroughly
researched, thoughtful and thought-provoking
analysis. Don't stay home on your own without it'
Mary Scott, *Everywoman*

Self-help/Therapy/Sexual Politics £7.99
ISBN 0 7043 4308 8

Stephanie Dowrick
**The Intimacy and Solitude
Self-Therapy Book**

In this companion volume to her bestselling book, *Intimacy and
Solitude*, Stephanie Dowrick guides us towards greater
fulfilment and joy through simple, effective self-therapy. She
does not provide formula answers, hoping they might fit.
Instead, using focused explorations and active meditations, she
inspires us to look afresh at our lives, enabling us to
strengthen ourselves and to find enrichment and reward in
solitude as well as intimacy.

'A treasure trove of exercises . . . This book should
be on any self-respecting bedside table. Read it.
Use it. Return to it as you would a familiar friend in
times of need' *Everywoman*

'A very, very good book . . . It speaks to me, to
modern experiences in relationships, much like a
profoundly satisfying conversation, late into the
evening with a very good friend. Thank you,
Stephanie' *Journal of Interprofessional Care*

Self Help/Therapy/Sexual Politics £7.99
ISBN 0 7043 4377 0

The Women's Press Handbook Series

The London Rape Crisis Centre
Sexual Violence: The Reality for Women
Third Edition

'If you or a friend have been raped then this book
will explain what you should expect from the police
and the courts, and what assistance is available to
you' *Guardian*

'Of real practical use to a wide range of health
workers' *Nursing Times*

'Might do a great deal to change the bigoted attitude
entrenched in so many people, not only men'
Nursing Mirror

The women of the London Rape Crisis Centre have been
working over a period of years supporting women who have
been raped or sexually assaulted. They discuss the politics of
rape and its use as a form of social control, as well as offering
full practical information about the medical and legal aspects,
and the emotional reactions of the woman involved, her friends
and family.

Addressed to women who have been raped, *Sexual Violence*
will also prove useful to professionals such as social workers
and legal advisers.

Health/Women's Studies £8.99
ISBN 0 7043 4436 X

The Women's Press Handbook Series

Kathy Nairne and Gerrilyn Smith
Dealing with Depression
Second Edition – Fully revised and updated

Why do so many women suffer from depression? How can we defend ourselves against this common problem and get out of what can quickly become a vicious circle?

Kathy Nairne and Gerrilyn Smith, both clinical psychologists, draw on their extensive professional experience together with the experiences of a wide range of women sufferers to offer this down-to-earth and comprehensive guide. From identifying the causes of depression to understanding the many forms it can take, from different ways of coping and recovering to evaluating the help available, here is an essential handbook for anyone who has experienced depression, either in themselves or others.

'A straightforward, practical guide . . . it explores its subject in depth' *Company*

'I can thoroughly recommend this practical, sympathetic and non-patronising book'
London Newspaper Group

'A soul-searing debut' *New Nation*

Health/Self Help £6.99
ISBN 0 7043 4443 2

Delcia McNeil
Bodywork Therapies for Women
A Guide

This informative guide examines the numerous bodywork
therapies available, with particular focus on their relevance to
women's physical and emotional health.

Including:

- Massage, Osteopathy
- Hypnotherapy, Rebirthing
- Traditional Chinese Medicine, Acupuncture
- Rolfing, Alexander Technique, Pilates
- Metaphysical Healing
- Bioenergetics, Gestalt
- Trager® Approach, Zero Balancing
- Yoga, Tai Chi and more.

Delcia McNeil examines each therapy in turn, outlining which
conditions it will help alleviate and explaining its theoretical
background and philosophy. She also clarifies what to expect at
each bodywork session and provides advice on how to find a
practitioner, as well as suggesting self-help techniques to try
at home.

Above all, McNeil advocates a holistic approach to health and
the body – highlighting the effectiveness of focused touch, non-
invasive treatments, sensitivity and intuition.

Health/Mind, Body, Spirit £8.99
ISBN 0 7043 4569 2